FAMILY AND FRIENDS IN **POLYMER CLAY**

Family and Friends in
POLYMER CLAY

MAUREEN CARLSON

NORTH LIGHT BOOKS
CINCINNATI, OHIO
www.nlbooks.com

ABOUT THE AUTHOR

Maureen Carlson is a teacher, writer, designer and storyclay teller. The common thread in everything is the ovenbaked polymer clay from which she creates her whimsical dolls and Wee Folk. While storytelling might not seem to be a logical extension of clay work, it is to Maureen, for her characters show such personality that they invite one's imagination to come alive. She frequently visits schools as a story-clay teller, where, as she creates a character in clay, she guides the classroom into an imaginary world where the little clay folk might live. By the end of an hour, there, sitting on the desk, is the finished star of the story.

Maureen says that if her own life were written like a fairy tale that it would begin with…

…Once upon a time there was a little pigtailed girl who lived on a Michigan dairy farm among the cats and the cows, and spent her days building her own things to play with from blocks of wood, leftover vegetables from the garden and scraps of fabric from momma's sewing basket. When she grew up, she traded the farm for a job as an elementary teacher, and then life as a "creative" wife and mother. Diapers and flower gardens, church meetings and organizational opportunities, outdoor craft shows and serendipitous books and acquaintances were all thrown into the life pot and stirred with enthusiasm and persistence. Twenty years later, she one day found herself to be an expert in polymer clay, so she and her husband Dan launched a mail order and teaching business called Wee Folk Creations. In 1999 Maureen realized a long-time dream when the Wee Folk Creations Retreat Center and School of Polymer Clay Arts opened along the banks of Sand Creek in Jordan, Minnesota.

Maureen has written for numerous craft magazines and has produced a series of instructional videotapes about polymer clay. You can find her What A Character Push Molds, Friar Folk, Sister Folk, Pippsywoggins, "Little Friends…From the Edge of Imagination" and "Wishing You…" fairies in craft and gift stores nationwide.

She has two grown daughters, a son-in-law and one grandson who frequently visit the rural home in Minnesota where Maureen survives the stress of frequent deadlines by digging in her gardens.

Bo

Family and Friends in Polymer Clay. Copyright © 2000 by Maureen Carlson. Manufactured in China. All rights reserved. The patterns and drawings in this book are for the personal use of the artist. By permission of author and publisher, they may either be hand-traced or photocopied to make single copies, but under no circumstances may they be resold or republished. It is permissible for the purchaser to use the designs contained herein and sell them at fairs, bazaars and craft shows.

No other part of this book may be reproduced in any form or by any electronic or mechanical means including information storage and retrieval systems without permission in writing from the publisher, except by a reviewer, who may quote brief passages in a review. Published by North Light Books, an imprint of F&W Publications, Inc., 1507 Dana Avenue, Cincinnati, Ohio, 45207. (800) 289-0963. First edition.

04 03 02 01 00   5 4 3 2 1

Library of Congress Cataloging-in-Publication Data

Carlson, Maureen.
    Family and friends in polymer clay. / Maureen Carlson.
        p.   cm.
    ISBN 0-89134-927-8 (pbk. : alk. paper)
    1. Polymer clay craft. 2. Sculpture—Technique. I. Title.
TT297.C27 2000   99-43672
731.4'2--dc21   CIP

Editors: Jane Friedman and Jennifer Long
Cover design: Kathy DeZarn
Interior design: Brian Roeth
Production artist: Tari Sasser
Production coordinator: Rachel Vater

The following are registered trademarks:
"Little Friends … From the Edge of Imagination"®
Pippsywoggins®
What A Character®
FIMO®
FIMO® Soft
Sculpey®
Storyclay®
Curly Craft®

The following are trademarked names:
Friar Folk™
Sister Folk™
"Wishing You …"™
FABRI-TAC™
Sculpey III™
Premo!™ Sculpey
Super Sculpey™
RAF-A-DOODLES™
CURLY HAIR™

ACKNOWLEDGMENTS

Without the courteous and efficient employees at National Camera and Video in Burnsville, Minnesota, this book would not be. Period. There are so many details to worry about when putting a book like this together. It was a pleasure not to have to worry about the film. I always felt hesitant as I laid the rolls of worried-over, struggled over, usually non-replaceable film on the counter. But, within hours the slides would be ready. I continue to be amazed. And grateful.

Any time a person makes a decision to do one thing, a decision is made to *not* do something else. To those business affiliates whose projects waited while I wrote this book, and who, in spite of that, have been unfailingly supportive, I am thankful. American Art Clay Company, Gift Connections, Craft Marketing Connections and Colorado Card and Curiosity Company, I'm ready now!

Life to me is an endlessly fascinating series of unrelated events that suddenly fall together into a perfectly planned puzzle. And sometimes one never knows how some of the pieces *ever* get there. But they do. For all of those people who had a part in putting my puzzle together, thanks for your time and energies. A few groups I would like to mention specifically: The Roy and Isa Peck extended family from Michigan, who so graciously got behind this project when I first started it, and who so willingly posed for me (note the Camp Peck T-shirts in some of the photos. I'm sorry that I couldn't use *all* of your pictures!); Karen Franklin of A. Franklin & Associates who connected me with North Light Books in the first place; the wonderful-to-work-with people at North Light Books, who have a gift for combining people skills with quality production (thanks especially to Jenny Long, Jane Friedman and Greg Albert); my fellow dollmakers from The Stone Soup Dollmakers Group, who keep reminding me of the necessity of play; and my family, including the Pecks, Tarrants, Carlsons and Boyers—*now* we'll have time to go to the Zoo!

DEDICATION

When you get off the ferry at the boat docks on Michigan's Mackinac Island, you are immediately transported into a misty, otherwhere world. The clip-clop of horse hooves and the squalling of seagulls float up and over the town and past the lovely old homes until they fade into silence along the wandering forested trails. It was in this place, on a lilac-shaded park bench at the end of Main Street, that I first met my husband Dan. Now, thirty-plus years later, I marvel that we were smart enough to know that he and I together were. And still are. And, because of that, many good things have happened in our lives. Thanks, Dan, for the behind-the-scene energy that keeps it all running.

TABLE OF CONTENTS

*T*he clay characters and dolls in this book make me smile. Still. Even though I watched them as they took shape from a lump of clay. Even though I chose their poses and clothes and ways of standing, and even though I know that they are not real, not really. I talk to them sometimes, too. Even though I know there is *no way* that they will answer back. Still…there *is* something about clay and the human form and the power of our imaginations that can reach out and make magic happen. I know, because it has happened to me.

When I first began to sculpt little people, I loved to craft and create things, but I had no special skills at art. I couldn't draw or paint or sculpt. Not really. But I had some clay that I'd been using to make mushrooms and flowers, so I found a picture of a character that I liked and tried to copy it. It wasn't good in a formal way. But people liked it. It made them smile and feel happy, or touched, and they wanted to learn to make characters, too. So I began to teach.

Once I got beyond simple funny faces, I realized that I didn't know what a face really looked like—and neither did many of my students. We'd never gone through the discipline of drawing or sculpting a human form over and over until we could *see* the shape of things. We'd never studied the actual skull upon which the face was built, and didn't really want to, but how could we make a nose or an eye or an ear if we didn't see or understand how it was put together?

That's when I began to take some classes and study drawing books and sculpting books and photographs of real people. I found quite a few that

were helpful (they are listed in the Resources), and some that I adored, but none that were written *just for me*, at the not-quite-beginner but definitely-not-classical stage. The book that I wanted had to be simple enough to be nonthreatening to my untrained eye, detailed enough to give me the basics that I really needed to know, and complete enough that I could actually make a number of characters from just the information in that book. Now, I hope, I have written that book.

As you look through this book, you will see a degree of exaggeration in all of my work. I like the way an

exaggerated portrait makes the characters knowable, accessible and familiar. In fact, a caricature, for that is what an exaggerated portrait is—sometimes allows us to see the person even more clearly than a more serious or realistic portrait would. What caricatures do is call attention to those features—both inner and outer—that make people uniquely themselves.

A good caricature also captures the mood of a person, and this is exaggerated as well. If the subject is bewildered, then the caricature is *really* bewildered. If the subject is happy, the caricature is *really* happy. If the mood is one of confusion or smugness, then it is endearingly so. This might sound like a description of cartoon characters, but what makes these sculptures caricatures and not cartoons is that there is something about each figure that captures the essence of an actual person. This is someone we know.

This book has three focal points: (1) learning to see, (2) learning to interpret what is seen through clay and (3) technical aspects of making a completed character. Learning to see sounds simple enough, but I have found that really seeing someone, seeing so that you can reproduce their image in an intentional manner, requires concentration and practice. There are millions of people in the world, yet each of their faces is different from every other person's. Why? What is it that makes each one unique? You can tell these people apart, but can you describe the differences? And, harder yet, can you reproduce these differences? Learning to *see* will help you whether you choose to create caricatures, cartoons or very realistic dolls and figures. The basic forms are the same for all. What makes the difference is only the degree of exaggeration.

I realize that making characters that look "almost real" can be quite a challenge, so, to ease you into it, first we will look at some general formulas for measuring faces and bodies. Once you are familiar with how the average person fits together, it will be easier for you to understand what makes a specific person look like himself or herself—instead of some "other." Since we began to recognize people, it has been only by unconsciously comparing one person's form to this generic "average" that we have ever recognized anyone at

all. Now we will begin to do that consciously, so that we can recreate those images.

The first actual caricatures that we make together, in chapter 6, will be rather generic ones. These will depend on accessories, size and coloring to create a likeness, rather than on the exaggeration of specific facial features. These caricatures will allow you to become familiar with some basic clay and sculpting techniques without having to worry about capturing a physical likeness. This chapter is especially for those of you who enjoy the technical aspects more than the measuring and comparing ones. In chapter 7 we'll sculpt a more disciplined face, one that requires a constant comparison with a specific image. I'll address the questions that you need to ask—as you sculpt—in order to make a character look like an actual person. Making portrait caricatures is a skill that takes practice, but it is so rewarding when you finally get it. It is such a thrill to focus in on the picture of a well-loved person, to concentrate on capturing that person's essence and then to hold the little replica in your hand. Looking back. Perhaps smiling. Slightly whimsical. Almost real enough to talk. You'll have to do it to know what I mean.

As you read this book, experiment with all of the styles or choose those that fit your interests and needs. Do scan through the whole book, though, as each chapter builds

on the one before it. If you run into a problem, chances are the answer is in an earlier—or later—chapter.

When I make clay caricatures of people, I know that there is a certain risk involved. After all, clay has the potential to make the character look so real that it can be spooky, offensive or hurtful. What I try to do is to capture a whimsical or smiling look that becomes fun. I look for those qualities that will allow for a gentle portrait—one that captures the emotional bond and, I hope, respect—that I share with that person. Then I present it with a smile—and hope for the best!

I do the same with this book. May it bring many hours of joyful pleasure to you and to your family and friends. So, let's begin! Take a deep breath. Give yourself permission to play, to have fun and to laugh a lot! Happy sculpting!

Maureen Carlson

Choosing a brand of polymer clay.

The colorful world of polymer clay offers many choices in hue, texture, strength and flexibility. Pictured in this playland are some of the common brands available in the United States: Cernit, Fimo, Premo! Sculpey and Sculpey SuperFlex. Though all polymer clays have the same basic properties, each has unique characteristics that make it the right choice for your specific application.

CHAPTER ONE

Understanding Polymer Clay: The Basics

WHY USE POLYMER CLAY?

Polymer clay was used to make the heads, hands and feet for all of the characters in this book. Flip through the pages and look at each face. Did you see any of them wink? That sounds like a silly question (well, it *is* a silly question!), but polymer clay does have a lifelike quality unmatched by any other clay. That is the first reason I use it.

The second reason for using polymer clay is the amount of detail possible. Choose a character from this book—any one with hands will do. Look at the lines in the fingers. Those are the same lines that I put into the clay when I made the hand. None of them were erased or added in the curing process.

Occasionally there will be unwanted cracking or surface pebbling (see page 120), but basically there are few surprises in surface changes. In fact, the clay is so responsive to detailing that unless I am careful, my fingerprints become a permanent part of each sculpture.

Add the fact that much of the clothing and hair in this book was made from polymer clay and you will see my third reason for using it. It is versatile. It comes in a whole rainbow of colors, all of which can be mixed to create new colors. It can be layered and patterned. It can be drilled, cut, sawed and sanded. It can be decorated with pencils, paints, powders and inks. It can be baked (cured), added to and then baked again. It can be simple in design or downright complex, quaint or breathtakingly elegant. In short, it responds to *your* imagination.

The final reason I use it is because it is accessible. If I have a home oven that heats to 275°F (130°C), a baking surface, a knife and a toothpick, I can create a character. A few extra supplies may make the process easier, but there are few essentials.

WHAT IS POLYMER CLAY?

So, we have this lifelike, detailed, versatile clay. But what is it? Well, it is not terra cotta, porcelain, stoneware or white art clay. All of these are traditional earth-based clays that must be fired in a kiln at temperatures ranging from 1830 to 2381°F (999–1305°C). Those temperatures would vaporize polymer clay! It is not an air-drying clay like Effaplast, Model Magic or Mexican Pottery Clay or an organic clay such as baking soda clay or flour clay. If polymer clay was left to air dry, it would crack and turn brittle; it would never become permanent. It is also not the same as a reusable modeling clay like Plasticene or Permoplast, since these can never be permanently hardened.

So what is polymer clay? It is a man-made clay composed of polyvinyl chloride (PVC) mixed with a plasticizer for flexibility, a filler for texture and pigments for color. It is cured to permanent hardness when baked in a home oven at about 275°F (130°C). Consult individual packages for baking directions.

Polymer clay is versatile. This piece, "My Grounding Place," shows some of the diverse uses for polymer clay. The tree-stump chair, quilt, doll, books, mug, flowers, flower pot and leaves are all made from polymer clay. Non-polymer clay items are the doll clothes and doll hair, the dragonfly, rocks, tendrils and the shell. The interior of the stump is aluminum foil (7½" × 9").

CHOOSING A BRAND OF POLYMER CLAY

There are many brands of polymer clay on the market including Cernit, Creall-therm, Elasticlay, FIMO, FIMO Soft, Gemcolor, Granitex, Polyform, Premo! Sculpey, Sculpey III, Sculpey SuperFlex and Super Sculpey. All of these clays have the same basic properties and, to my knowledge, can be intermixed. Each one is unique in terms of the amount and type of filler and pigment added. These additives affect the color, the texture, the flexibility, the shelf life, the strength, the opacity, its response to warmth and its blending characteristics. I suggest you become familiar with the different brands of polymer clay, and then experiment to see which has the properties most important to you.

I traditionally do most of my work in FIMO, so many of the pieces in this book will be made with FIMO. FIMO is a stiff clay, which I like for the stability it gives the characters as I build them. Others prefer a softer clay that requires less conditioning, such as Cernit or Premo! Sculpey. They then use tools that allow them to touch the clay as little as possible to prevent it from overwarming and becoming too soft. Which brand of clay you use depends on your technique, the heat and humidity of the environment and even the amount of body heat in your hands. It's a personal choice.

PURCHASING AND STORING POLYMER CLAY

Polymer clay does have a shelf life, which means the clay will become firmer as it sits on the shelf. For this reason it is best to buy fresh clay. If possible, buy from a supplier who frequently orders new supplies. If you have to use hard or old clay, don't despair. I have never found a package of properly stored polymer clay that I could not bring to working consistency through warmth, patience or the addition of a softening agent. Notice, however, the words "properly stored."

Make friends with a food processor! Clay mixed in a food processor comes out looking like cottage cheese and is warm and ready for kneading.

I add those words because I have found packages of clay harder on one side than on the other. When chopped and mixed, this clay has little hard lumps that do not smoosh into a workable putty, no matter what! These packages have been exposed to excess heat somewhere in the shipping-and-storage cycle and have become partially baked.

Once you decide which brand of clay to use, read the package instructions. Each brand has specific baking and safety recommendations. Store the clay at room temperature away from direct light, in the original package or plastic bag. Avoid foam or rigid plastic containers, since clay sometimes reacts with those compounds. Avoid porous materials such as untreated cardboard, paper towels or fabric. These may soak up the plasticizer and leave the clay less pliable. (Note: Some people who want firmer clay leach the plasticizer from the clay by layering thin sheets of it with absorbent materials.)

CONDITIONING

You will need to warm and condition the clay before using it. Open the package to see how hard the clay is. Hold a piece in your hand until it is warm and then knead it. If it becomes workable (pliable, uniform consistency) immediately, then you merely have to fold and twist it for a few minutes before starting to work.

SAFETY CONSIDERATIONS

Many brands of polymer clay carry the following notice: For children eight years of age and older. Use under adult supervision. Use a domestic oven thermometer to observe temperature. Do not exceed maximum baking time/temperature or harmful gases may be produced. Do not place material in the mouth.

This warning may be elaborated upon by following these rules:

1. Keep tools used for clay separate from tools used for food.
2. Bake in the center of the oven, where there are fewer hot spots.
3. Bake on an insulated or doubled pan to prevent bottom burning.
4. After use, clean hands with soap and water or a waterless hand cleaner.
5. If you develop an allergic reaction to polymer clay, discontinue use or wear gloves.

Most polymer clay brands sold in the United States are certified as nontoxic by the Arts & Crafts Materials Institute. They are also labeled as conforming to ASTM D-4236. It is my understanding that this means they are safe to use as long as the manufacturer's recommendations are followed. Some people choose to use a separate oven in which to bake their polymer clay pieces. This is not because of recommendations by the manufacturer or the testing institute, but rather for the following reasons:

1. They don't like the smell of baking clay, and a separate oven allows them to bake outside or in a garage where the smell is more diffused.
2. They dislike using chemical products in an oven also used for food.
3. They bake what amounts to commercial quantities of clay, resulting in more fumes and more oven residue.

Working with hard polymer clay. If polymer clay is hard or crumbly after warming it, mix in a softer clay, diluent or kneading medium such as Mix Quick. Knead and twist and knead again until the clay is uniform in consistency and color. Here we see Carl rolling a rope of Mix Quick and FIMO through some crumbly pieces to pick them up and mix them in. This sculpture is reminiscent of a night in 1986 when the real Carl came for a visit and ended up kneading a ton of clay for me. Lesson: If you use one of the stiffer clays, make friends with someone with big, warm hands.

PRACTICAL CONSIDERATIONS

If you are so conscious of safety warnings that you overreact and underbake your pieces, you may end up with very weak pieces that break easily. This gives a bad name to polymer clay artwork as being temporary and doughlike. Please be careful when you use polymer clay so as not to burn it, but do bake it adequately. When polymer clay is adequately baked there is fusion of the polychloride grains, resulting in a hard plastic product. Inadequate baking means inadequate fusion, and thus very fragile items.

BAKING

I have experimented with many different baking temperatures and times. For thorough baking I recommend that you bake pieces at the longest time listed on the package at the highest recommended temperature, and then cool them in the oven. Some manufacturers recommend baking fifteen minutes for every ¼" thickness.

I bake polymer clay in a convection oven in which the fan constantly circulates the air to provide uniform baking. I have had more even results since I began using a convection oven, but I still never leave items baking unattended. Many variables affect results, such as the mass of the item, the number of items on the baking sheet, the distance from the clay to the top and bottom of the oven, the brand of clay used, the type of armature, the thickness of the clay and even sometimes the color of the clay.

If you don't have a convection oven, you can use a regular oven, either gas or electric. If your pieces are small, a toaster oven is suitable. Don't crowd pieces in any oven, as that may result in uneven baking and hot spots. You may want to shield the top of your pieces with a tent made from baking paper or baking parchment.

Thorough baking is essential for strength. To ensure uniform and thorough baking, it is best to have an armature inside your polymer clay pieces. This cuts down on the thickness of the piece, thus ensuring it bakes all the way through. It also reduces cracking caused by uneven baking. Here we see the armatures used inside two Santas.

CARE OF FINISHED PIECES

Once a polymer clay piece is adequately baked, it is considered a permanent product. If you want it to become a family heirloom, treat it like the high-quality piece that it is. Most brands are quite strong, but most will also break if treated roughly. I suggest you handle it like fine porcelain: Don't drop it. Even though it frequently bounces, don't push your luck. Don't bend it (unless your brand of clay was made to bend, such as Sculpey Flex or Elasticlay). Polymer clay may be washed with soap and water, but don't put it in the dishwasher, as both hot water and the dry cycle may cause it to warp. Don't display it in direct sunlight, as it may fade or deteriorate.

Bake at highest recommended temperature for strength. My cousin Elaine is here with a special message: Use the correct oven temperature when baking your character! If you bake at a low heat, you may produce a weak product due to inadequate fusion of the microscopic particles. I use a separate oven thermometer to test the temperature, and I bake at the highest temperature recommended on the package of polymer clay.

Tools and Supplies

First, a story ... Once, a very long time ago, there lived a magical sculptor. This sculptor created clay figures that truly seemed to breathe. Many people came to watch the sculptor work. It was often reported that if one glanced away for a moment the figure would seem to move ever so slightly, and would be in a new position when the person looked back. Everyone who came to watch the figure take shape knew that they were in the presence of a master.

One of the sculptor's most frequent visitors was a young girl who wanted more than anything in the world to be able to sculpt like her hero. As she watched, intent upon the sculptor's every move, she noticed that the master chose a certain tool more than any other. Believing that this tool held some special qualities, she snuck into his studio one night and stole it away.

Early the next morning, the girl eagerly took the tool and began to sculpt. She was anxious to see how this wonderful, magical tool would improve her skills. Of course, her results were the same as before. Nothing about her had changed.

Meanwhile, on the other side of the village, the master, deep in the process of creation, reached for his favorite tool. Not finding it, he frowned and then shrugged as he turned to his remaining tools. He chose one, eyed it closely, rubbed it between his fingers and then smiled with satisfaction as he returned to his work—using not the tool, but its handle.

This story illustrates a simple point: there is no magic tool, except for the mind. Skill does not come with the ownership of a tool: It comes from knowing what you want to accomplish with it. Once you are comfortable with your skills, you will find that even the most elementary of tools can be used to create amazing things.

Complicated tools are not essential. Making characters from polymer clay needn't be complicated. This character was made using only the pictured tools and supplies. Included are a rolling pin, knife, toothpicks, flat brush with a smooth pointed handle, aluminum foil, ceramic tile, a sturdy wire, wire cutters and waterless hand cleaner.

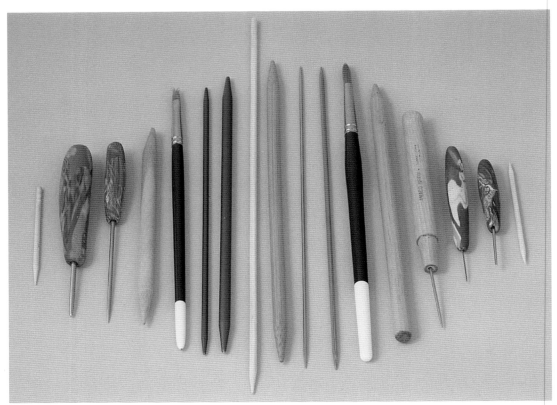

Collect pointed tools. Search your junk drawer, sewing basket and art supply store for various tool shapes and sizes. Notice that I made polymer clay handles for some of the needles.

THE SHORT LIST: BARE ESSENTIALS

This list includes enough tools to get you started.

- knife (paring knife, utility blade)
- knife for children
- something round, pointed and sharp (needle tool, toothpick, darning needle, knitting needle)
- something round, pointed and dull (tapestry needle, larger knitting needle, crochet hook, clay shaper/taper point, friller tool, wood or plastic modeling tools, paintbrush handles)
- wire or stick for an armature (toothpick, piece of coat hanger, dowel, popsickle stick, florist wire, fence wire)
- baking surface (baking pan, foil, ceramic tile, index card)
- an oven (gas or electric, toaster oven, convection oven)
- aluminum foil

THE LONGER LIST

When you have experimented and discovered you might really get into this sculpting "thing," you'll find the following tools useful. Check under Resources for hard to find items.

- fingernail tools (the head of a nail or commercial nail tool)
- roller for flattening clay for clothing (rolling pin, brayer, pasta machine, smooth glass bottle, acrylic rod, 1" or 2" wooden dowel)
- wire cutters
- food processor
- acrylic paint
- paint brushes
- transparent paints
- baking paper or parchment
- colored powders or chalks
- waterless hand cleaner
- very sharp blades (utility knife, craft blade, NuBlade, wallpaper scraper blade, tissue blade)

The "comes-in-handy" list. If you really get into making characters, try some of these tools. Recently I invested in a pair of Lineman Wire Cutters, available at hardware stores. I don't know how I did without them!

Rolling sheets of clay. If you make characters with clay clothing, a pasta machine makes it easier to create uniform sheets of clay. The pasta machine is one of my indispensable tools. But if you don't have one, take heart! For ten years I used a plain old rolling pin, and I made hundreds of characters.

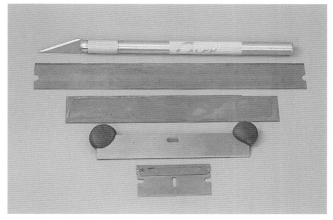

Very sharp blades. The three long blades allow for clean, thin slicing of clay millefiori designs used for patterned clay clothing. The ones pictured are a wallpaper scraper replacement blade, a tissue blade and a NuBlade. The single-edged razor blade is great for making clean, quick cuts in small spaces. The craft blade is great for intricate pattern cutting.

MATERIALS FOR DOLL-MAKING

If you will be dressing your caricatures in fabric clothes, collect, collect, collect. Rescue bits of this and that from worn-out old clothes, garage sales, antique shops and your attic. Collecting these supplies can be as much fun as making the dolls!

- fabric for wrapping armatures (old sweatsuits, craft batting)
- material for stuffing (polyester stuffing, cotton puffs, raw cotton, plastic grocery bags)
- fibers for hair (yarn, wool, shredded paper or plastic, telephone wire, frayed fabric, rafia, moss)
- fabric for clothing
- glue (FabriTac or hot glue)
- sewing supplies
- scissors
- forceps for stuffing

The fabric closet. Feast your eyes on this variety of fabrics and fibers that can be used for stuffing, hair and clothing. Becoming a dollmaker can be a fiberholics dream, as you now have an excuse to buy lots of luscious, but little, pieces of enchantment. And little bits of scrap that are of no use for bigger projects are just the right size for dolls.

CHAPTER TWO

The Face as a Puzzle: Spatial Relationships

IDENTIFICATION BY COMPARISON

My two friends, represented by the dolls in these pictures, have much in common. They each have two eyes, two ears, mouth, nose, chin, lively hair (with which I took liberty!) and adventurous dispositions. I started both caricatures with the same basic shapes and I used similar sculpting techniques, but they didn't end up looking alike. Why? What is it that makes one person—or one doll— look different from another? How can our faces, which are composed of basic parts that are so similar to everyone else's, still be so unique?

Artists have been asking these questions ever since they first tried to record a human likeness. Fortunately for us, rules of proportion have been developed for measuring and comparing the human form. Our bodies and faces are so consistent with each other that these rules of proportion, if followed, are a good starting point for any caricature. It's this basic proportion of the human form that makes us look so similar and yet so different. We are so refined at comparing one person's features with another's that we unconsciously detect the differences when someone's nose or mouth is even a fraction of an inch higher or lower than the average person's. This constant comparison with the average allows us to identify people. The trick is to bring that knowledge to the surface so we can exaggerate the unique qualities.

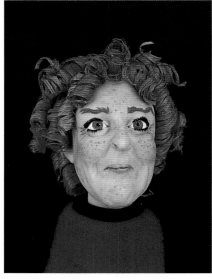

Ruth. FIMO with RAF-A-DOODLES curled raffia hair; head measures 2¾" from chin to top of head. (See the real Ruth on page 23.)

AnaBel. FIMO with dyed sheepskin hair; head measures 2½" from chin to top of head. (See the real AnaBel on page 93.)

NO SUCH THING AS IDEAL

Before we begin, indulge me as I give my classroom lecture titled "No such thing as ideal!" From dealing with my own emotions and with those of students, I know that comparison studies of the human face and form can trigger feelings of inadequacy and "wrongness." Society pressures us to conform our faces and bodies to an ideal so much that we stop celebrating the wonderful variety of the real. And real is what caricatures— and life—are all about!

Please understand that measurements of proportion are not intended to be a standard to measure up to. They are just average measurements, and I, for one, have never wanted to

be average. (Well, maybe for awhile in my teens! How about you?)

The face we call *average* for the purpose of study is just that. Average. It is for discussion and instruction purposes only. You may share some measurements in common, but some you will not. Those differences will make your face great for caricature. They are what make you distinctively you. With that said, let's create an average person whom we will call Sam. (Note: These proportions are for adults. The eyes of children are lower on the head than the eyes of adults. Our faces continually change proportion from the time we are born until sometime in late adolescence.)

Average Sam

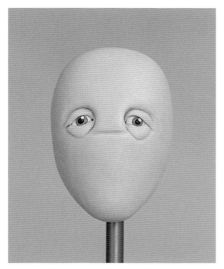

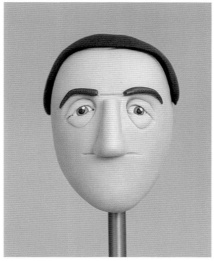

The halfway point. For our average adult Sam, if a square is drawn around his head we will find that, in a front view, his head is two-thirds as wide as it is long. The center of his eye is at or just above the halfway line between the top of his head and the bottom of his chin.

The rule of thirds. Locate the top of the forehead, where the hairline starts. The face divides into three equal parts: hairline to center of brow, brow to base of nose and base of nose to chin.

His face is five eyes wide at the eyeline.

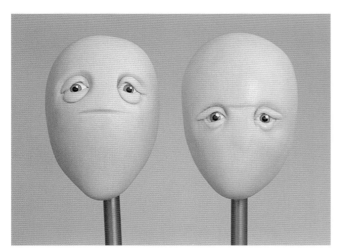

Placing his eyes higher will make his face look longer. Placing them lower will give him a small face with childlike proportions.

Look at what happens when we try to divide his high-eyes face and low-eyes face into thirds. On the left his eyes are on the eyebrow line. So where do we put his eyebrows? On the right we see that if we put his eyebrows on the eyebrow line, it makes him look very surprised. The lesson? The parts of the face are like a puzzle: Change in one part affects the others.

The eyebrows are now repositioned to match the placement of the eyes. But what would happen if we move the noses around? Right now, all three versions rest on the second one-third marker line, or the average nose line.

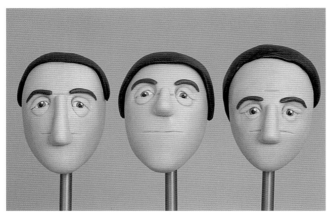

Here I mixed the noses around and ended up with none of them sitting on the nose line. That means none of these versions of Sam is average. Fun, though, aren't they? Which appeals to you most?

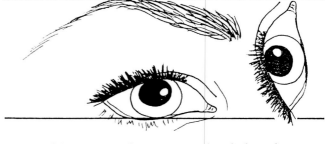

The top of the average eyebrow is one eye length above the eye.

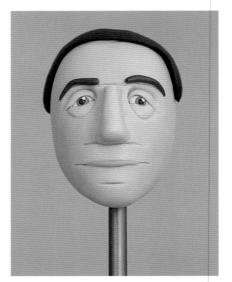

Bottom one-third in thirds. Sam's nose is back to average placement. I divided the bottom third of his face into three equal parts. The center of the average, unsmiling mouth is one-third down from the base of the nose.

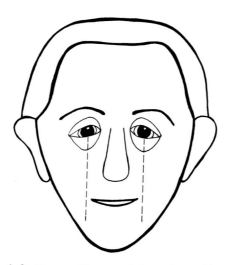

left: His unsmiling mouth is nearly as wide as the distance between his pupils.
right: If a triangle is drawn to connect the corners of his eyes with the bottom center of his mouth, it will be an equilateral triangle.

In the other two versions of Sam the lower third of his face is average, but the proportions of the other two parts make him look unusual. The version on the left has a very short forehead and a long nose in comparison to the average Sam. The version on the right has a very high forehead and a short nose. Average Sam would be less easy to identify than these two, as there is nothing about him to make his face unusual or memorable.

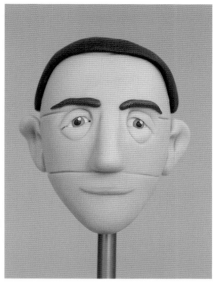

Nose-to-eye. Average ears fit between the bottom of the average nose and the top of the average eyes.

Since the features of these two Sams aren't on the average placement lines, the bottom-of-nose-to-top-of-eye guideline makes the ears on the left very large and those on the right very small.

I've smoothed the lines and given the Sams a little smile. Can you still see and identify what makes each unique? Remember we are comparing the two on the right to the average one on the left.

Look what happens when the noses and mouths are moved from their "average" lines. Now all three faces are distinctive compared to an average face and can more easily be described. None is average, but all are charming (in my opinion). It's hard to believe all of these characters have the same basic head shape. See how much difference the feature placement creates?

Using Graphs for Feature Placement

I measured the heads of four dolls and made a graph for each, which you see placed behind them in the pictures. The graphs are marked to show the hairline, forehead line, eye line and nose line. I was surprised when I measured them to find that nos. 1, 2 and 3 all have their eyes pretty much on the half line. Only no. 4 deviates. Notice the noses on my dolls: I must be partial to noses that make a statement! Note that the nose line is marked at the point where the base of the nose touches the face, near the nostrils. It is not measured at the tip of the nose, which in nos. 1 and 3 dips much lower than the actual nose line.

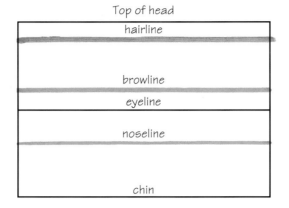

Graph for placement of average features.

CREATING IN YOUR OWN IMAGE

Figure making is a very revealing and personal type of work. Making charts for your figures often gives information about how you see the world. These charts showed me that all of my dolls tend to have low foreheads. I think this is because I've always thought my own forehead was too high; as a result I usually wear bangs: I seldom see my forehead! Do I overcompensate when I make dolls? There is truth in the saying we create art in our own image.

1. Fear/Need. It's hard to determine the top of Fear's head by the picture, since his hat makes his head look tall, but I could tell by feeling his head that his forehead is not one-third of his face. If I were to treat Fear/Need as a real person and make a caricature of him, I would emphasize his small, close-together eyes that accentuate his wider-than-average nose and mouth. The triangular shape of his chin and jaw is also accentuated by the triangular upsweep of his eyebrows. (Super Sculpey; painted eyes, sculpted and painted eyebrows, hand-woven wool hat; head measures 2½" from base of chin to top of bare head.)

2. Prankster Pratt. Prankster Pratt has almost identical feature placement as Fear, but the angles (eyebrows, mouth) go in opposite directions. In a caricature of him those angles would be exaggerated even more. The shape of his face and long ears would also be distinctive. (FIMO; painted eyes, appliqued and sculptured eyebrows, yarn hair; head measures 2¼" from base of chin to top of unwigged head.)

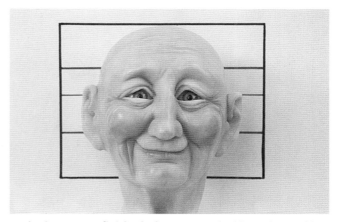

3. Troll. Both the Troll and Zinnia Rose, No. 4, show a feature placement uncommon among real people. The center third of their faces (the nose section) is longer than either the lower or upper third. And we won't even mention those ears! (FIMO blended with Mix Quick; clay applique eyes, yarn hair; unwigged head measures 2¼" from base of chin to top of head.)

4. Zinnia Rose, unfinished. If Zinnia Rose had hair, she would have a very low forehead, indeed! Notice I didn't mark any hairline for her. With figures and dolls you can often give the illusion of forehead height when you add hair or hats. (Cernit with Glastic acrylic eyes; head measures 3" from base of chin to top of head.)

NOW FOR A REAL DOLL

Let's see how the rules of eyes-on-the-half-line and face-divided-into-thirds apply to a real person. This is my adventuresome friend Ruth. Let's give her a big hand for allowing me to analyze her face in public. Thank you, Ruth!

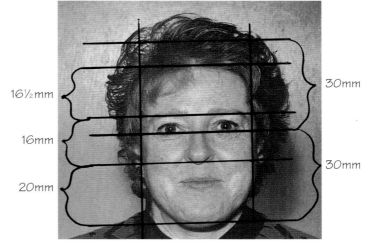

To help analyze Ruth's face, I put a piece of clear acetate over her picture and drew a graph to mark her feature placement. If your perception is very keen you may "see" her face without the graph, but I've found that my eyes often deceive me. So for me this technique is very helpful. The graph tells me Ruth's nose is higher than average, making the lower third of her face longer than either of the other two-thirds. I can also see that her face is slightly narrower than average—less than five eyes wide.

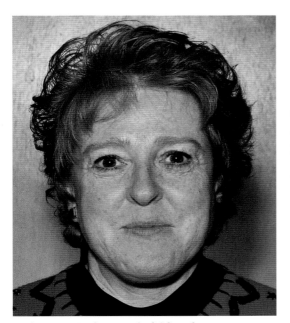

Smile pretty! Ruth is wonderful for a first caricature; her distinctive freckles and red hair are easy to duplicate and right away give a clue that *this is Ruth.*

Placing the features on paper forces me to see where they are and saves me time when I begin with the clay. If I go directly to the clay, I tend to create more serious, realistic clay caricatures rather than exaggerated ones. I believe this is because my mind attempts to recreate what I actually *see* in the picture, rather than *translating* what I see as a caricature. Playing with the features on paper helps me loosen up and create more accurate exaggerations. Then I work from the drawn caricature instead of the photo to get more whimsical results.

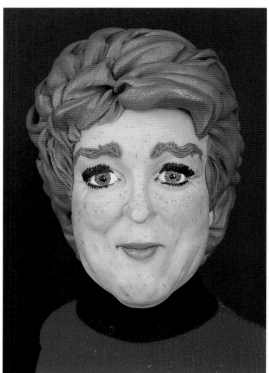

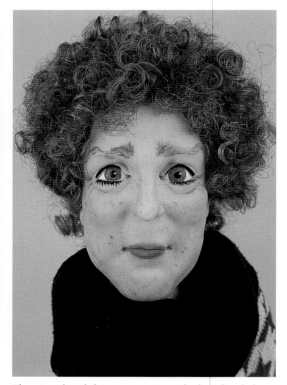

This is the first Ruth caricature I made. I think it captures her, but it's too serious. Why? I think I looked at the photo too much and got caught up in making it look real. I did shorten her forehead and exaggerate the size of her already large eyes. Her nose is quite narrow, so to exaggerate it I made it narrower. (FIMO with a small amount of Cernit; sculpted hair, eyelashes and eyebrows, painted eyes; head measures 3¼" from chin to top of head.)

Then I sculpted this one—trying to be less detailed. The lips are tiny, pink clay appliques I pressed in place and then sculpted slightly. I think the lip line is a little too low. A tiny fraction of an inch is critical when capturing likenesses, especially on tiny faces. (FIMO with a small amount of Cernit; CURLY HAIR polypropylene filament, painted eyes and eyebrows; head measures 2½" from the chin to top of head.)

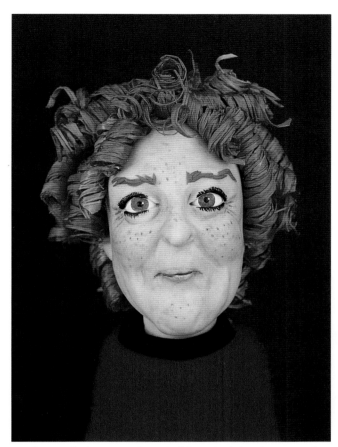

TIP FROM A CARTOONIST

Here's tip that I read in Dick Gautier's book, *Drawing and Cartooning 1001 Caricatures*: "Try drawing on tracing paper or using a lightbox to trace copies and recreate features. Then shift the layers of paper around to see where the features are best placed. How far can you move a feature without losing the resemblance?"

DON'T FORGET TO CHECK THE PROFILE

Let's go back to average-guy Sam.

We see in the photo that Sam is paired with a more realistic version of the average guy—this one called Joe. From the front we see that both faces conform to the rules of

1. Eyes on the half line
2. Face divided into thirds for placement of the nose, eyebrows and hairline

Finally I made this one and just had fun. I had the placement of her features clearly in mind. This is my favorite. Her lips are lightly sculpted, mostly an indented line and then painted. I like the exaggeration of her features—just enough to be fun! (FIMO with Cernit; RAF-A-DOODLES natural curled raffia; head measures 2¾" from chin to top of head.)

THANK YOU

I am indebted to the authors of the drawing and anatomy books that are listed in the Resources section on page 125 for giving me specific tools and information with which to learn to see faces. I am especially grateful to Lenn Redman, author of *How to Draw Caricatures*, for his head-in-a-square and graph system which I have adapted for use in this book.

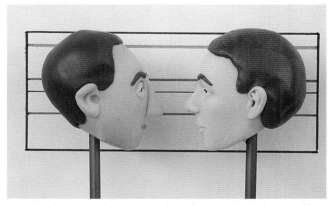

But what happens when we turn both faces to check their profiles? Sam is no longer average. Now we see that his sloping forehead and receding chin make him stand out from the average face—represented now by Joe. Sam's profile would give the caricature artist something to work with!

CHAPTER THREE

The Basic Face: Learning to See the Shape of Things

FOLLOWING A MAP

Once I heard about two old men, neighbors, who agreed on most everything except how to take a Sunday afternoon drive. Fred believed the best way to do it was to just get up from the dinner table, hop in the car and head down the road. Wherever his whimsy took him was the perfect direction to go. Everywhere he met interesting people, and each Sunday drive was an adventure.

George believed the best way to take a drive was to anticipate the day in advance and to plan what he wanted to see or whom he wanted to visit. Then, only after he had his map firmly in hand, would he hop into his car and head down the road. And for him, too, every Sunday drive was an adventure.

I can relate to both Fred and George when I think about my attitude toward sculpting. Some days I want to be like Fred and just head on down that road without a map. I experiment to see what face comes out of the clay to visit with me. Sometimes it ends up being someone I know, and sometimes it doesn't, but the whole experience is rewarding. Other days, like George, I have a specific destination. I try very hard to create a specific person, and I find that following the map (that person's face) is necessary to reach that goal. This method is often frustrating, but it is exhilarating when I reach my goal.

Shandella. (FIMO conditioned with Mix Quick; clay applique eyes and eyebrows, CURLY HAIR continuous polypropylene filament, wrapped wire armature body; head measures 2¾" from tip of chin to top of head.)

READING MAPS, SEEING FACES

My point in sharing this story is to give you permission to skip this chapter if you aren't ready—or in the mood—for another chapter that deals with maps or, in this case, faces. In this chapter we will be taking some time to look at the specific shapes that make up a face, and we will be learning to read them for the clues that make one face different from another. Some of my friends have kindly agreed to let us look at them "up close and personal" in order to demonstrate just a few of the many variations of those basic shapes. Use this chapter to teach yourself to *see* the details. If you are anxious to get your hands into the clay and just begin, feel free to skip ahead to chapter 4. But remember that this chapter is here for you when you need it.

Going Beyond the Symbols

You can see from Shandella that changing the shape of even one facial feature drastically alters a person's appearance. Imagine how important it is to get the shapes right when creating a caricature that must resemble someone. Any old shape won't do.

That particular nose may look great, but it may belong to someone else! Unless you really learn to *see* what you are looking at, you may alter a shape without even realizing that you are doing so.

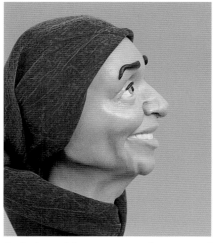  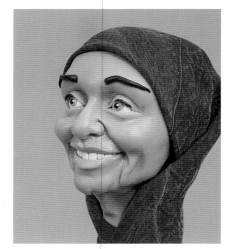

Sculpting without a map. When I created Shandella I was spontaneous, like Fred. I made a face and let it take me where it would. And look what happened: Shandella emerged full of life.

 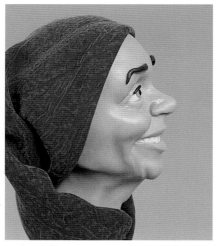 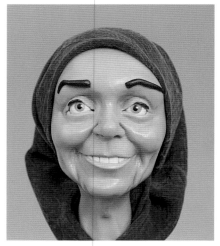

But then I wondered what she would look like with a different nose, so I borrowed one from someone else.

And how about a different mouth? Does she like this one?

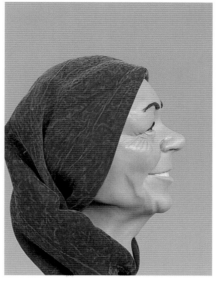

Her eyes looked wide and youthful. I decided to give her an older, wiser look, so I made her eyes droop a little.

Last of all I gave her flatter cheeks to reflect the new persona. Hmm. If you change the shapes do you change the person? Is it still Shandella?

One way to get beyond the symbols and see the actual shape is to consciously ask yourself the following questions:

1. What is the shape?
2. Where does it start?
3. What direction does it go?
4. Where does it stop?
5. How does it relate to the features around it?

If possible, look closely at the people around you as you read this chapter. Photos flatten subjects into two-dimensional images. I've provided three-quarters and profile views of some of the subjects so you can get a clearer image of the dimensional aspect of their features. But the real thing, in person, is the best sculptural teacher. So look around you.

We'll start with the whole-head shape, for that is what we recognize about a person from a distance. And just as we did in the previous chapter, we'll look at an average head first so we have a form for comparison.

Symbols for the nose. It is obvious this is a drawing of a nose. We've learned to recognize this mark as a symbol for the concept *nose*. When we make a caricature we are tempted to go into our mental storehouse of symbols, look up the file marked *nose*, pick one that we like and put it into place. But that doesn't work for caricatures. Noses come in many more shapes and sizes than that.

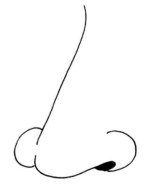

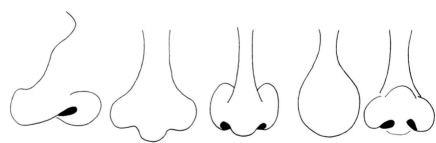

Now we have more choices. But even these are not enough. Each person's nose is distinctive, and so are her mouth, eyes, ears and head shape.

Head Shape

The guidelines for average head shape are:

• When placed in a square, we see that, in a profile view, the head is slightly longer than it is wide.

• The ear falls behind the half line of the head.

• The neck meets the back of the skull at a point behind the ears, about level with the mouth.

• The front of the face is built on a slight curve, with the chin and forehead receding just slightly from the front line of the face.

• The jaw angles from the chin back toward the ear and then, at a point slightly lower than the mouth, the jaw turns upward and rises to end in front of the ear.

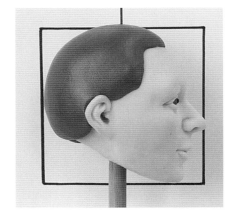

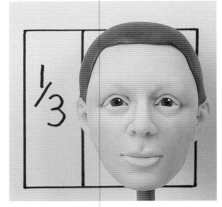

When placed in a square, we see the front of the average head is two-thirds as wide as it is long. The lower cheeks taper in a gentle curve toward the chin.

Uriah's face very closely fits the average guidelines for head shape. At age twelve, he is old enough to have grown past the proportions of a child's face, but he still hasn't developed the bony eyebrow ridge common in men.

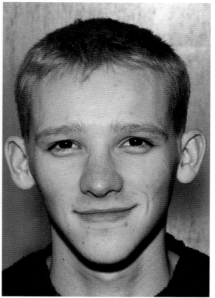

Maureen's and Michael's faces reveal opposites in terms of shape. Maureen's is very square, while Michael's is triangular. Both of these would be easy caricatures because of the distinctive shapes.

Outline face shapes for Uriah, Maureen and Michael will give you a clue where to start if you were sculpting them in clay. Determine the basic head shape first, and form that in clay. Then go to the individual parts.

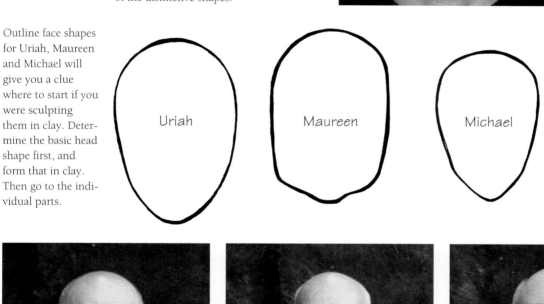

Uriah

Maureen

Michael

Of course it is always easiest to look at head shapes if we can find heads without any hair! Luckily, bald heads run in my father's family. Three of my cousins, Carl, Richard and Robert, demonstrate how the shapes of heads vary widely.

Their profiles are just as distinctive.

Drawing the shapes may help you see them. If you could capture these shapes in clay, you would be well on your way to making their caricatures.

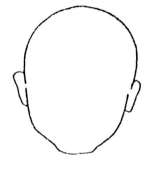 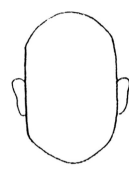 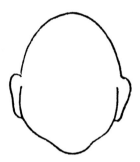

Carl   Richard   Robert

PRINCIPLES FOR CARICATURE
Remember for caricatures that the guiding principle is: If a feature is bigger than the average, make it even bigger, or wider or farther apart. If it is smaller than the average, make it even smaller or closer together or narrower.

Mouths

The mouth area is from the base of the nose down to the chin and sideways to both cheeks. This unit is a whole, since movement in any part will change the rest. There are visual clues in this area about the character's emotions so, next to the eyes, it's the most important indicator of personality. Guidelines for the average mouth are:

- The unsmiling mouth is one-third down from the nose.
- The unsmiling mouth is not quite as wide as the distance between the pupils.
- The upper lip protrudes slightly over the lower lip.

It is important to get pictures from various angles that show the mouth position in relation to other features. A front view will not give you a rounded picture—and that's what sculpture is: Round.

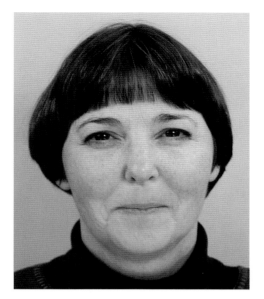

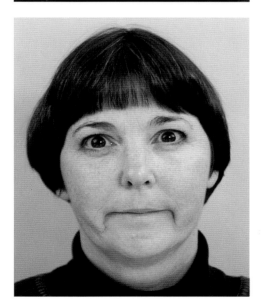

See how changeable Lu's face is? In the broad-smiling example, the upper lip rises closer to the nose and the lips flatten as they stretch from cheek to cheek. The nose widens. The lip corners deepen into the cheek curve, resulting in a deeper wrinkle pointing toward the chin. The eyes and cheeks change to correspond with each mouth expression. In the two above photos, the cheeks are like the shape of a full-bodied comma, and the upward-moving cheeks cause the eyes to crinkle and partially close. In the bottom photo, the cheeks are flatter, like two lima beans, and the eyes remain wide open.

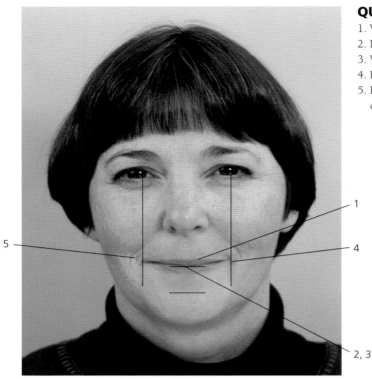

QUESTIONS TO ASK:

1. What shape is the upper lip? Lower lip?
2. Does the mouth open on the average mouth line?
3. What is the shape of the line between the lips?
4. How wide is the mouth compared with the pupils?
5. How does the mouth relate to the curve of the cheeks?

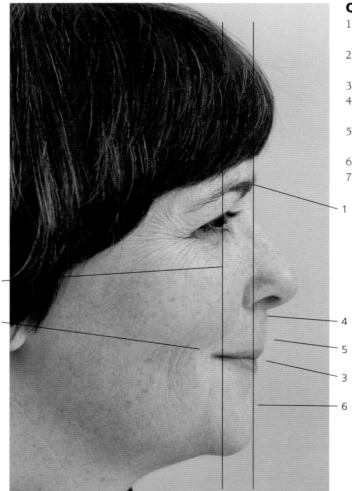

QUESTIONS TO ASK:

1. Where are the lips in relation to the chin and fore head?
2. How deep are the lips in relation to the front of the eye?
3. Which lip protrudes?
4. Where does the skin above the upper lip touch the nose?
5. What is the upper-lip shape between the mouth and nose?
6. What is the shape between the mouth and the chin?
7. How do the lips relate to the curve of the cheeks?

Noses

The nose comes in many shapes, but the following general description of the average nose will help you analyze your subject's nose.

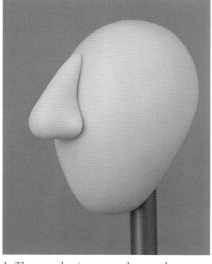

1. The nose begins as an elongated pyramid that lies against the face.

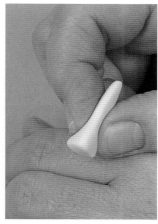

2. Pinching the pyramid to taper the top two-thirds of it will result in two wings from which the nostrils can be built.

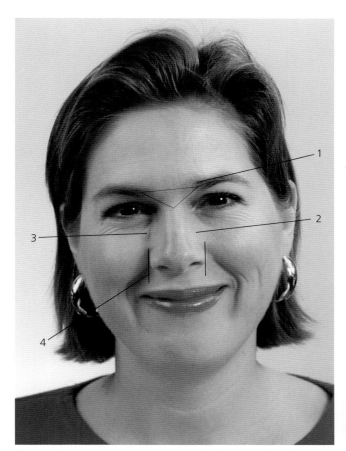

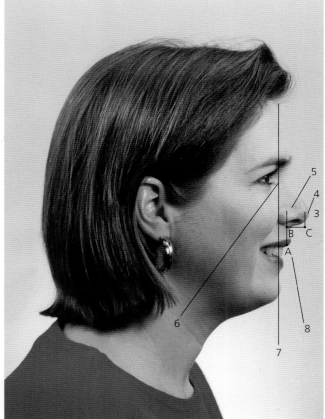

(Thanks, Darcy, for letting us look so closely at your face!)
1. The top of the nose blends into the brow in a triangle shape.
2. The sides of the nose blend into the cheeks like a ski slope.
3. Sometimes, if the person is smiling, a little gully will be at the end of the slope and then the hill of the cheek rises in front of it.
4. At its broadest point, the average nose is eye width.

3. The nostrils point down, not out to the side.
4. The tip of the nose is rounded like the end of an egg.
5. The septum joins the nose to the upper lip, with one-third of the nose being behind the front lip line.
6. Compare the bridge of the nose with the depth of the nostrils and the corners of the mouth.
7. Compare the bridge of the nose with the depth of the eyes and the position of the chin and forehead.
8. Lines AB and BC are equal.

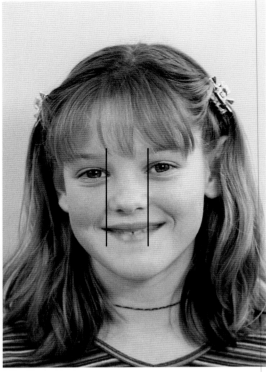

Amy's nose tilts up from the upper lip. The top dips into a gentle curve. This makes her nose look small in the profile view. But, as we can see in the front view, it is as wide as the average nose, which is the width of one eye or the same as the distance between the eyes.

Compare the angles and width of Bob's nose with Amy's. When doing a caricature, it is very important to see the shapes and angles of your subject's features.

Cheeks

Cheeks at rest always remind me of flat lima beans against the side of the face. But when the person smiles, they curve into rounded commas.

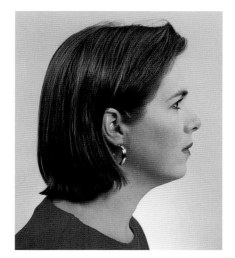

In Darcy's pictures, first we see an unsmiling mouth with flat cheeks, and then a slight smile creating a small curve in her cheek. Last is a broad smile with a deep comma shape at the point where her smile intersects the cheek. Compare the front of her eye in each picture with the depth of her smile and the depth of the cheek curve. Notice the area directly under the eye in each picture. The shape changes with the uplift of her cheeks.

Notice the full, soft roundness of the top of Darcy's cheeks as compared with Bob's, even though both are smiling broadly.

When Bob smiles the curve of his cheek sharpens and the wrinkles at the corners of the mouth and around the nose deepen. The top of his cheeks slope in toward the eye socket and then slope up to meet the sides of the nose. Look at the spot just above the nostrils where the cheeks join the nose. The cheek curves smoothly from the plane of the front of the face to that of the side, where the cheeks meet the ear. If I were making a caricature of Bob I would accentuate those crinkly, deepset eyes and the arrow shape of his nose.

Eyes

Eyes have always been the hardest part of the face for me to sculpt. I think that is because there are so many shapes that come together at the eye. The nose, the cheek, the cheekbone, the ridge of the eye socket and the brow ridge all affect how we perceive the eye. Some general guidelines for the shape of the average eye are:

- The adult eye is at or just above the half line of the head.
- The shapes of the eye are determined by the nearly perfect roundness of the eyeball, the iris and the pupil.
- The lids fit around the eyeball like curved window shades.
- Only the top lid actually opens and closes.
- The lids fit around the curve of the eyeball, with the inner corner starting just before the white of the eyeball.
- The inner corner is a small pinkish-white notch. In the Asian eye, the inner corner is hidden by a fold of skin.
- The inner corner is lower than the outer corner.
- It is rare to see the whole round iris unless a person is excited.
- The outside corner of the eyelid is often covered by drooping skin, especially in the older eye.

In these pictures of Patty and Fred, we see how important it is to have more than one view of a person's eyes. Some spatial relationships are not visible with just the front view.

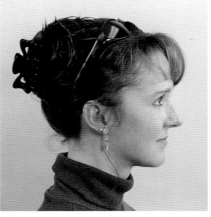

1. How large are their eyes compared with their face? (The average face is five eyes across at the eyeline, with the space between the eyes equal to one eye.)
2. What is the curve of the lower lid?
3. What is the curve of the upper lid?
4. How close is the eye to the eyebrow?
5. What is the shape of the eyebrow? Where does it start? Where does it end? What point is highest? Lowest?
6. How much of the upper lid shows?
7. What is the shape under the eye? Is there a pouch or a dark circle?

1. In a three-quarters view, what is the shape in the area between the eye and the eyebrow?
2. How much does the eyebrow ridge extend beyond the middle of the eye? Beyond the far side of the eye?

Ears

The basic shape is a *C* with a *Y* and a keyhole sitting on top of it.

Ears, too, come in many shapes and sizes, though the basic shape is the same. The average ear is as long as the distance from the top of the eye to the bottom of the nose. But some are higher. Some are lower. Some lay flat to the head. Some stick out. Some are different on one side of the head than they are on the other. I heard once that ears are as identifiable as fingerprints. I don't know if that is true, but as I look at the ears of my friends in this chapter, I see that they are all alike, yet different in subtle ways.

Study the shape of the ear so that it is clear in your mind. If you can't see it, you can't sculpt it! And that is a good sentence with which to end this chapter. For it holds true for all of the parts of the face. If you can't see the general shape of it with your eyes closed, you will probably have a hard time sculpting it. So, as you practice making faces in the next chapter, keep coming back to this chapter to see what the basic shapes are and how those shapes fit together to make each face unique.

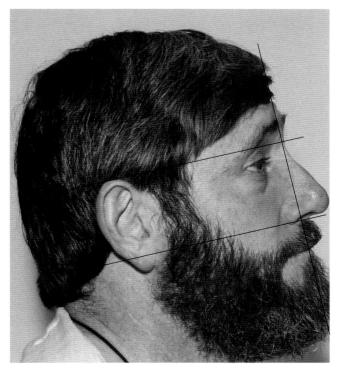

The average ear fits between the top of the eye and the bottom of the nose. Dan's ears are slightly longer than average. However, at first glance it looks as though his ear is much lower than the bottom of his nose. Notice that his head is tilted back, which throws off the horizontal lines. When using a photo, be sure and check the angle of the head before assuming that someone's ears are low or high.

CHAPTER FOUR

Make a Funny Face: Cartoon Characters

The actual techniques needed to sculpt a face are very simple. They can be lumped together into two basic sculpting methods: (1) add-on and (2) push in, pull out and take away; and one general technique: blend and smooth. If you can do those three things, you can make a face! This chapter and chapter 7 will teach you how to use and refine these techniques. To make this chapter both fun and relaxing for you and me, we will be practicing on cartoon faces, not ones that must look like a certain person. Faces that are caricatures of real people will come later, after you have mastered the basic skills.

BAKING

Polymer clay can be baked in a regular oven, toaster oven or convection oven—not a microwave. Bake in the center of the oven, not too close to the top, bottom or sides, since reflected heat can burn. Place clay head on a baking sheet or ceramic tile or propped up in an ovenproof dish such as a ceramic coffee mug. Follow directions on the polymer clay package for exact time and temperature, as different brands have different requirements.

Add-on Face

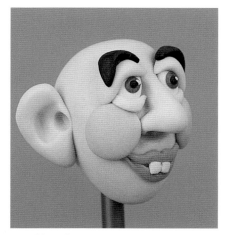

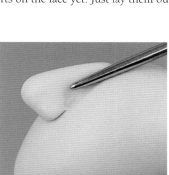

An add-on face represents the simplest method of sculpting. All features are shaped in clay and then added in layers. The only trick is to achieve the shape and size you desire for each facial feature.

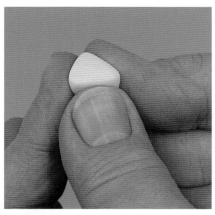

I'll demonstrate making a specific shape with the nose. Use your fingers to press one side of the nose into a triangle shape. This will automatically make the rest of the ball into a pyramid. Alter the length and form by stretching or compressing it.

Use your finger and then a brush to pat and blend the surface. The trick to using the brush is to first blend a small amount of clay into the bristles of the brush so it is slightly stiff, yet still soft. Use repetitive brushing motions to drag and pat small amounts of clay into place. The brush can get into areas, such as around the nostrils, where your fingers are too big.

For this first face, practice making pieces similar to the ones pictured, starting each in the shape of a very smooth ball. Don't place the parts on the face yet. Just lay them out on the table, like pieces of a puzzle.

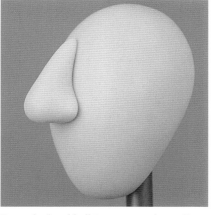

Form the head ball into an egg shape. Press the nose on the front of the face.

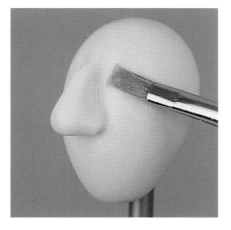

Blend and smooth. Use a smooth, blunt needle tool to blend one edge of the nose into the clay of the face. Don't grab too much of the nose clay with your tool, only the edge. This technique feels a little bit like spreading a very thin layer of frosting onto a tender cake. If you push too hard you will gouge the surface. If you push too softly you will not camouflage the joining edge. Also use the needle tool to indent nostrils into the base of the nose.

Finish the face by adding the rest of the features in this order: bottom lip, teeth, upper lip, cheeks, white eyeballs, blue iris, black pupil, white highlight, lower eyelid, upper eyelid, eyebrow and ears. Press the pieces on firmly enough so they don't move when bumped. There is no need for glue or slip when attaching unbaked pieces of polymer clay to each other.

Push In, Pull Out and Take Away

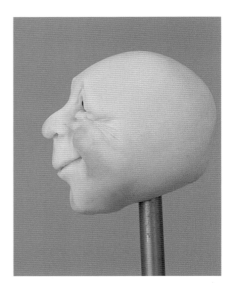

This character represents a face created by making a head shape and then pushing in and pulling out existing clay to create the features. No clay was added, except for the black eyeballs. This is a more complicated method than the add-on face, so for this first lesson on push in/pull out, I will just demonstrate the creation of a mouth.

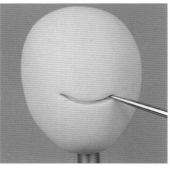

Use a blunt needle tool to indent the corners of the mouth. This pushes them into a deeper plane than the front of the face.

Use a sharp needle tool to press/draw a mouth. By press/draw, I mean use a pressing and dragging motion with the edge of the needle.

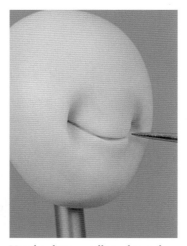

Use the sharp needle tool to redefine the line of the mouth.

Right: This character's nose, ears, eyes and eyelids are add-ons; the rest of his face is push in/pull out. (Head is 2¼" from base of chin to top of head.)

Blend and smooth. Use your fingers or the clay brush tool to smooth the edges of the smile and remove the tool marks. (In general, if your fingers are smooth and if they will fit the space, use your fingers. A smooth thumb is my favorite tool.)

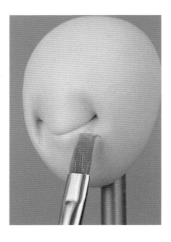

Make a Funny Face

Now that you have learned the three basic techniques, you are ready to create a more complicated face that is a blend of all three techniques.

ARMATURES

An armature is the supporting material inside of a sculpture. The first two heads I created for this chapter were only 1⅜" tall, so I made them from a solid ball of polymer clay. Generally, solid balls of this size are safe to create, although sometimes they will crack during baking, because the inside of the ball is not heating up as fast as the outside.

For larger heads I recommend a wire-and-foil armature. The size of wire and amount of foil are determined by finished head size. The wire should be sturdy enough to provide solid support for the head weight. Sometimes I use a toothpick or a wooden dowel for support, but the wire gives more flexibility for the final positioning of the neck. If the head is 1¾" tall or smaller, a single wire should be fine. For larger heads, double the wire.

The pictured wire is 14-gauge fence wire, similar to clothes-hanger wire. Loop the wire at the top to prevent the head from twisting as you work on it. Cover the loop with crumpled foil until it resembles the desired shape for the head. Plan on the foil head being ¼" smaller on all sides than the finished head. Notice that the foil is not haphazardly crumpled onto the wire. I have been careful to create the back of the head shorter than the front, which is designated by the chin. Sometimes I shape the foil like a skull, which I will demonstrate in chapter 7.

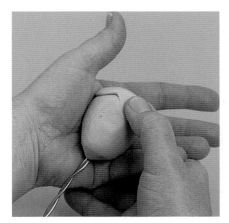

Press flat pancakes of clay uniformly over the surface of the foil, keeping track of the front of the face.

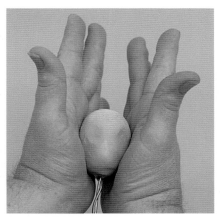

Use your palms to press and smooth the head into a firm egg shape.

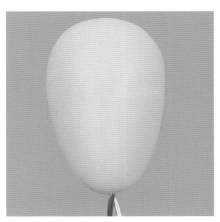

Be careful at this stage to get the head shape as uniform as possible. If you start with a bumpy or lopsided shape, it will be hard to create a balanced head. Features do not cover up the basic head shape!

Use a sharp needle tool to press/draw in the mouth line.

Check the mouth from the side to be sure the front of the face is curved, not flat. The mouth should be visible from the side.

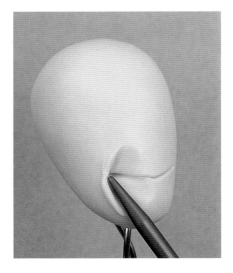

Use a blunt needle tool or clay shaper tool to deepen the corners of the mouth and create a cheek line.

Press the tool against the mouth surface to curve it into the deeper plane of the face.

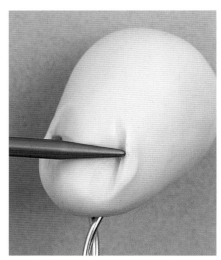

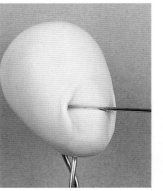

Redefine the line of the mouth.

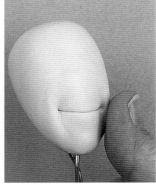

Smooth and blend the corners using your thumb and/or the clay brush tool.

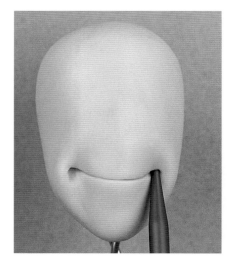

Pull the corners sideways a bit to create some expression to the mouth.

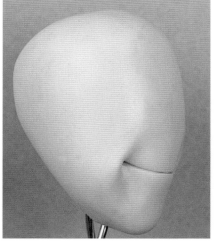

Check the profile view to see if the lines are deep enough into the cheeks.

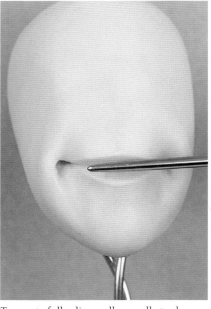

To create fuller lips, roll a needle tool down across the lower lip and up across the upper one.

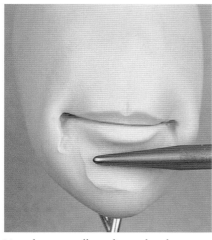

Use a larger needle tool or a clay shaper to press the dip into the top of the upper lip. Roll the tool under the lower lip to create more depth to that area.

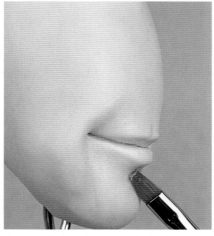

Use the clay brush to smooth the lip area.

TRY ON SOME NOSES

The shape and position of the nose will make a big difference in the appearance of your character. Create several noses and "try them on" to see which one appeals to you. The black eyeballs are temporary ones to help you determine the nose placement.

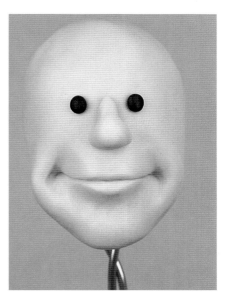

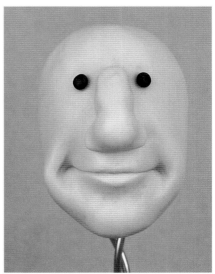

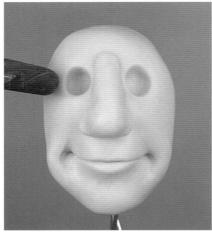

Once you have chosen the nose and positioned it, use a round tool, such as this baked polymer clay form, to create eye sockets.

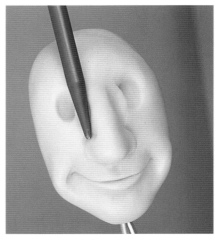

Use your thumb to blend the top of the nose into the forehead.

Shape and blend the sides of the nose into the cheeks. This also begins to define the bulge of the nostrils.

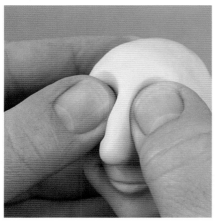

Use your thumbs or a smooth, round tool to smooth the eye sockets and to narrow the bridge of the nose.

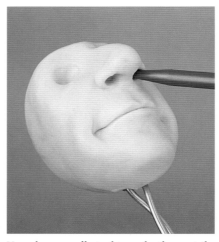

Use a large needle tool to make the nostril holes. Push the tool in and then pull it slightly sideways to get a bulge. The nostrils begin right next to the skin of the upper lip area—not at the tip of the nose.

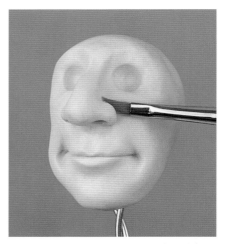

Use the clay brush tool to smooth and further define the nostril area.

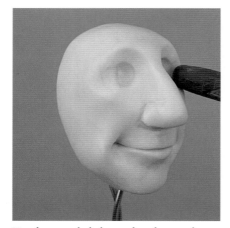

Use the rounded clay tool to deepen the outside edge of the eye sockets.

Use a sharp needle tool to mark the corners of the eyes. Make two white clay balls the same size. Drop the balls into the eye sockets, being sure that both are at the same depth. Press on equal-sized brown balls for each iris, tiny black ones for the pupils and really tiny ones for the highlight. Be sure that the highlights are positioned the same on each eye.

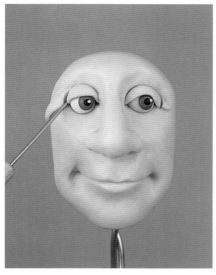

Roll two long comma shapes. Flatten each slightly, and then lay one over each eye. The eyelid should fit from eye corner to eye corner like a small window shade. If it is too big, use a needle tool to trim it.

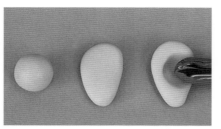

Form simple ears from two equal balls of clay. Form each into a teardrop shape. Flatten each one, and then hollow out the middle.

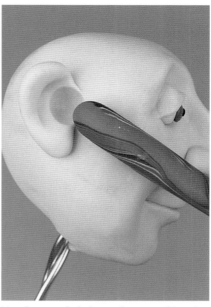

Use the rounded clay tool or round brush handle to press the center of the ear in to head.

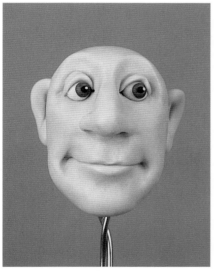

You can stop at this point—you have created a real character. But with a little more work, you can create a character with even more personality.

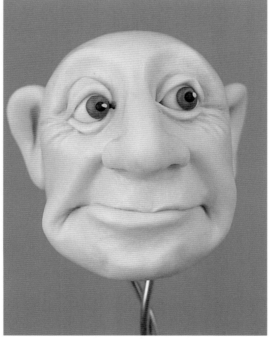

One of the wonderful things about clay is that it isn't done until you decide it is—and then it is! It is alterable at each step along the way. Two simple changes are needed to change the previous character into this one—who looks like he really has something to say.

ADD EXPRESSION TO THE EYES

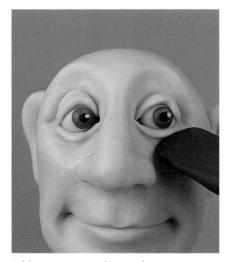

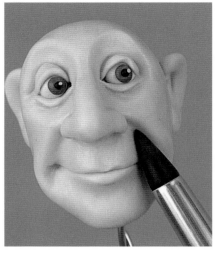

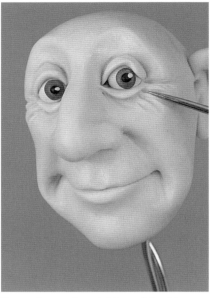

Add expression to the eyes by creating a lower eyelid. This lid is not added on but pressed in with the edge of a curved clay tool. Create several tools of this shape in different sizes to help make various curved lines.

Press the cheeks higher on the face. This creates the impression of a wider smile and more crinkly eyes. (Look in the mirror with a straight face. Smile broadly. See how the cheeks move toward your eyes and become rounder in the center? Notice how your eyes become less wide?)

To emphasize the crinkling of the skin around the eyes, use a sharp needle tool to press in crow's feet.

OPENING THE MOUTH

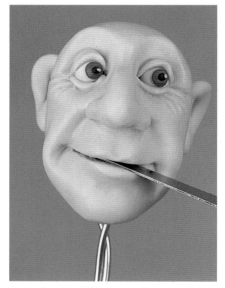

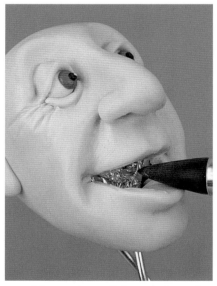

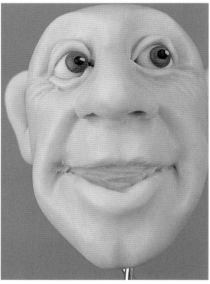

Open the mouth by cutting between the lips with a sharp knife. Don't be afraid! If you wreck it, you can always use the blend- and-smooth technique to recreate the mouth. You *can*!

Use a blunt tool to pull down the lower lip, and then smooth out the inside of the mouth.

Use a blunt needle tool and a brush to pack clay into the mouth to cover the exposed foil.

ADDING TEETH

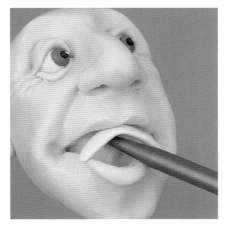

Open the character's mouth again. Flatten a strip of white clay and insert it into the mouth.

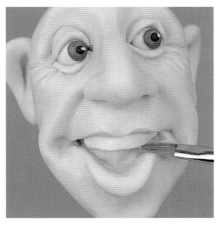

Use a brush to position edges. Use a needle tool and a knife to cut in teeth lines.

Reposition the character's mouth as if he were talking. Play with different positions and expressions. Open and close the mouth. Press it sideways. Pull out the chin. Move it back. You can stop now, or go on to the next step for a new look.

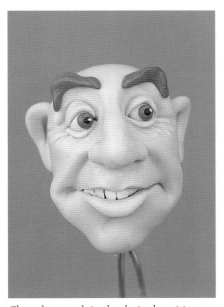

Close the mouth in the desired position. For eyebrows, press on a rope of brown clay.

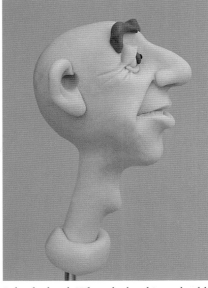

Bake the head. When the head is cool, add a ring of clay for the neck. Blend and feather the edges. Bake the head again.

Now our character has teeth and a little color in his face, plus hair and a hat. Almost comes to life, doesn't he?

Add a transparent coat of paint for blush and lip color. Glue on hair.

Freckle-Faced Girl: Add-on Sculpting

You probably know by now there is no one right way to sculpt a face. When you begin a caricature you decide the end results, so you choose methods to give you the desired outcome. If I am trying to capture the caricature of a specific person, I most often use the add-on method for the basic facial feature, which I will demonstrate with the freckle-faced girl. In the following steps you will see that the smoothing and blending techniques are the same as those demonstrated with previous characters—only the way of adding the features is different.

Freckle-Faced Girl. (FIMO head with Mix Quick added for softness; painted features; head is 2½" tall from base of chin to top of head; the completed doll is 15" tall)

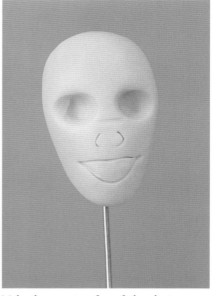

Make the armature from foil and wire. Smooth base clay onto the armature to create the desired head shape. Draw in features. Press in eye sockets.

FALSE TEETH

Choose a wooden dowel slightly smaller than the width of the jaw. Wrap the dowel with foil. Make two strips of white clay. Use a curved, concave tool to press in the shape of the teeth. (You can make a similar tool from polymer clay, and then bake it.) Lay the two strips over each other like false teeth. Bake according to directions.

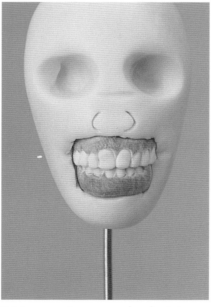

Paint gums using rouge-colored paint. Press teeth into place over the mouth lines, pressing them to the desired depth.

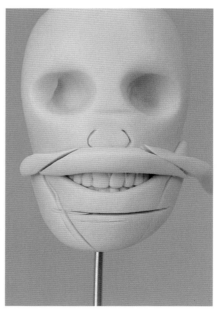

Flatten strips of clay to mimic the thickness of the lips. Place strips over the teeth, cutting them to fit from nose to chin to both sides of the cheeks.

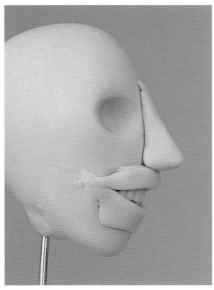

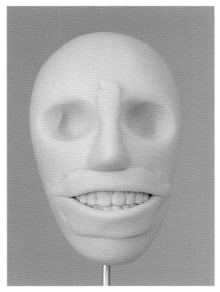

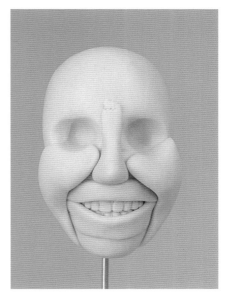

Remove trimmings. Set the nose in place above the lip pieces.

Press the edges of lip pieces to taper them slightly and to blend them into the face.

Determine the shape of the cheeks from ear to eye to nose to lips to jaw. Create two pieces the same size and shape. Press into place. Start with a ball and flatten it into a teardrop and then into a comma shape slightly fatter in the middle. Notice (1) a wing of clay blends into the sides of the nose, just above the nostrils, (2) the top of the cheek mimics the circle of the eye socket and (3) the curve of the comma surrounds the corners of the mouth.

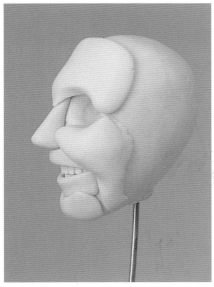

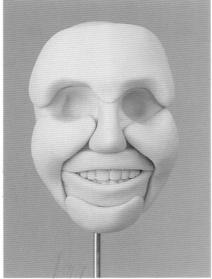

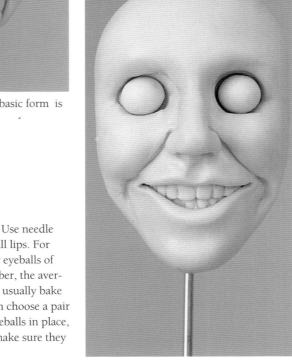

The sides of the cheeks blend back toward the ears; they should be thinner at the outside edges. After blending and smoothing, there should be no ridge along the edge of the outer cheek. Add a forehead piece to bring the brow area beyond the nose bridge. The sides of this piece end just beyond the eye socket. Add a chin piece to bring it out to the desired place. The average chin aligns with the brow area.

Check all pieces to see if the basic form is what you want.

Blend and smooth all pieces. Use needle tools and a brush to create full lips. For eyeballs, bake two white clay eyeballs of the appropriate size. Remember, the average head is five eyes across. I usually bake various pairs of eyes and then choose a pair that best fits. Press cooled eyeballs in place, checking from all angles to make sure they are even.

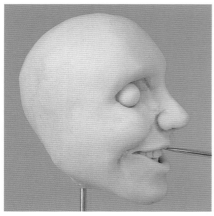

Since both the teeth and eyeballs are pre-baked, you can push them in or pull them out to reposition them without harming their shape.

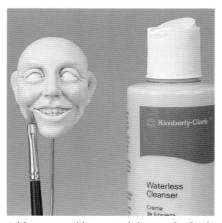

Add upper and lower eyelids. For the final smoothing, place a small amount of waterless hand cleaner on a brush. Use this to smooth and blend all remaining rough areas. Bake head for 20 minutes at the recommended temperature.

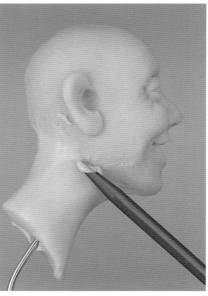

Cool the head, and then blend the neck into the head, using a needle tool and brush to blend and feather the edges. Do final smoothing with waterless hand cleaner. Bake the head at the highest temperature and for the longest time recommended on the package.

PAINTING THE HEAD

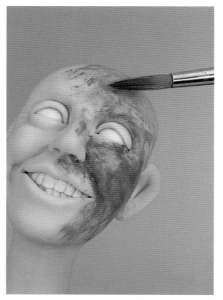

Brush a coat of brown paint over the cooled head, but don't allow it to dry. (Use a transparent blending color, acrylic paint or thick watercolor paint.)

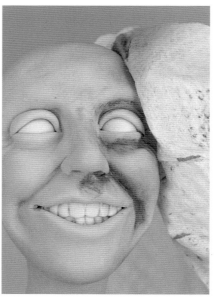

Use a soft cloth to quickly wipe away all extra paint, leaving just a light coating to highlight the depth of the wrinkles, etc.

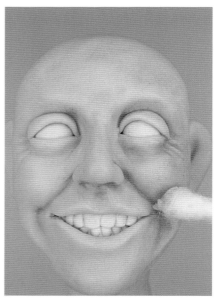

Use a cotton swab to remove paint from hard-to-reach areas.

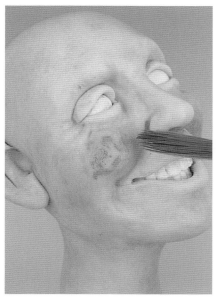

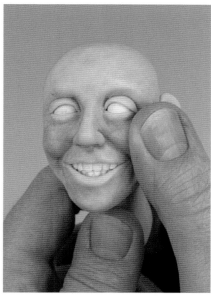

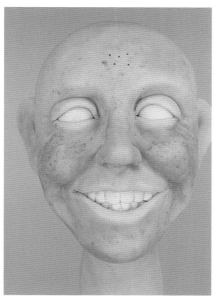

Dab rouge-colored paint onto cheeks. (Note: Sometimes when baking the clay will crack where the clay is thin or stretched. Not until after this face was painted did I notice tiny cracks at the mouth corners. One solution is to fill them with raw clay and rebake at the highest recommended temperature for at least 20 minutes. Sometimes you will need to do this several times before it is adequately camouflaged.)

Remove excess rouge with a cloth or brush. Dab wet cheek with your thumb to blend color.

Dot on brown acrylic paint for freckles. While paint is still wet, dab with damp finger to feather out the dots and make them less regular. Add lip color to cheeks and any gum area that might have lost paint during the sculpting process.

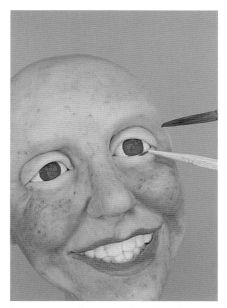

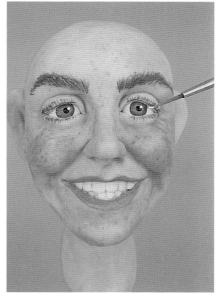

To paint eyes, first paint the colored iris. Paint as though the perfect circle of the iris extends beyond the eyelids. If any paint gets on the eyelid, wait until it dries and then remove it with a toothpick.

To create eyelashes and eyebrows, use a nearly dry brush in a light lifting stroke to paint one hair at a time. Dot on a white highlight to the same spot on each eye.

Gallery Section

I used a combination of the techniques in this chapter to create three caricatures of my friend Lu.

Lu is a wonderful subject for a beginning caricature, as her distinctive hair alone is nearly enough to proclaim, "This is Lu!" Other easy-to-caricature features are her crinkled, chocolate-brown eyes, straight-across eyebrows, freckles, narrow, uplifted nose and heart-shaped face.

 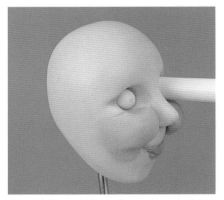 

This first caricature is fairly simple add-on sculpting. (FIMO; hair is a mix of terra cotta and anthracite FIMO; head is 1¾" from base of chin to top of head.)

I mixed the base flesh clay with pink clay until I achieved two pink shades, from which I formed the lips and cheeks. The lips were pressed in place and then sculpted lightly. The cheeks were blended into the face only on the outside edges. I used a rounded tool to press out the eye sockets, and then inserted raw white balls of clay.

Black balls were pressed on the center of each eye for a combination iris/pupil. I frequently do this with very small eyes to eliminate some of the detail. After adding comma-shaped eyelids both top and bottom, I added extra clay to the brow to build up that area.

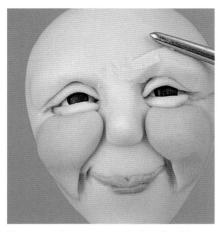 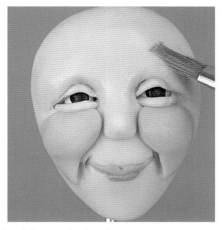 

The extra clay was smoothed with a blunt tool and then with a brush.

Clay eyebrows are added. After baking, the white highlight is painted onto each eye. The freckles and eyeliner are also painted with acrylic paint.

 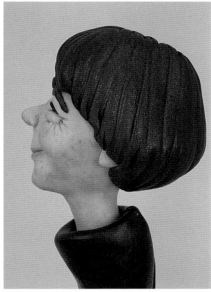

The second caricature has push-in, pull-out lips and cheeks with an added-on nose, clay eyes in three colors (white, brown and black), clay eye liner and clay eyebrows. The lips, cheeks and freckles were painted after the face was baked. I think this caricature captures Lu's spirit and, of course, that great hair! But the mouth is a bit too far away from the too-big nose, and the face is too narrow at the cheek line. The anthracite FIMO has silver metallic particles in it, which accounts for the shiny hair. (FIMO; hair is a mix of terra cotta and Anthracite FIMO; head is 1⅞" from base of chin to top of head.)

 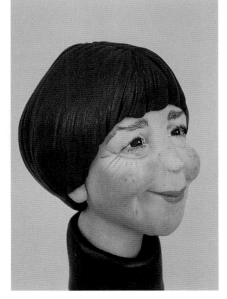

I spent the most time on the last caricature, which is my favorite of the three. I made her eyes and cheeks bigger and her nose smaller than they are in real life. From the profile view, you can see that the bridge of her nose and brow on the caricature are flatter than on her real face. For a more de-tailed, true-to-life caricature I could have built up that area to more closely mimic the actual shape, but I decided against that. This is a caricature, not a portrait, and I was happy with it as it was. Isn't she cute? (Head is 2¼" from base of chin to top of head.)

CHAPTER FIVE

Body Proportions: Caricaturing the Body

I f you were following along in chapter 4, you now have at least two or three completed clay heads. Have you gone so far as to strike up a conversation with any of your clay creations? If so, I bet they are saying, "Give us a body. Give us a body!" And that's just what we will do in this chapter—talk about and make some bodies.

If you are making a cartoon character based on an imaginary image in your head, you can use any body shape and size that appeals to you. But if you are making caricatures of real people, or character dolls that are meant to be realistic, you should pay close attention to the principles of body proportion. But sometimes it's hard to even *see* what a person's body proportions are if you don't understand something about those principles. For instance, how does that person's body compare with the average body? Is it taller or shorter? Wider or skinnier? Longer or shorter legs? And so on. It is these comparisons that allow us to identify and recognize people and enable you to successfully re-create their character in clay.

Fortunately, we have a set of average-proportion guidelines for studying bodies. Once you understand them, it will be easier to look at your characters and choose how to interpret that character.

Do you recognize these characters? We "met" most of them in earlier chapters. They don't look the same when seen next to larger or smaller creations, do they? Your work area will begin to look strange if you don't start putting some bodies with those heads!

PRINCIPLES OF PROPORTION

Please note that the proportion guidelines in this chapter are relevant whether you make characters like the ones represented here or ones of your own unique style. The human body is the human body is the human body, so no matter how or in what material you interpret it, the same basic proportional guidelines apply. For examples of these principles interpreted in doll form, see chapter 8.

IDEALIZED FORM

Few people are exactly the same as the "average" character on which the proportional guidelines are based. Please consider whether you are trying to fit everyone, including your clay creations and dolls, into an idealized form. Each of us is unique; don't add to the pervasive "sameness" we seem to strive for in modern culture by insisting there is *one way* for a person, or a clay creation, to be proportioned.

Head Size

AS A MEASURE FOR HEIGHT

One of the most common ways to understand average human body proportion is to compare the height of the body with how many heads tall that person is. The drawing books I studied based the proportion charts on an average adult figure that was either 7½ or 8 heads tall. One even stated that for purposes of fashion or grace the figure might be nine heads tall. If you intend to do babies or children, it is especially important that you pay attention to the relationship between the body and the size of the head, since these relationships give us visual clues to the child's age. Newborns are about four heads tall, while, by age 8, the average child is nearly 6½ heads tall.

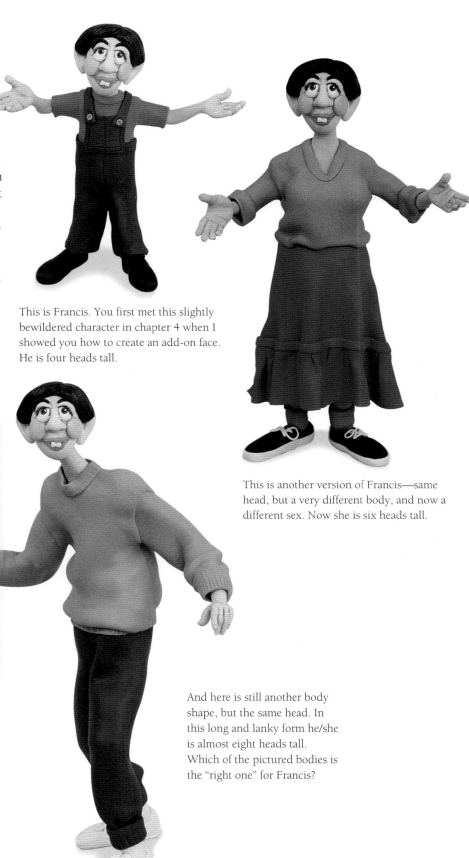

This is Francis. You first met this slightly bewildered character in chapter 4 when I showed you how to create an add-on face. He is four heads tall.

BODY CARICATURES

When doing body caricatures, the principle is the same as that for faces: If one of your subject's features is larger than or farther apart than the average, make it even larger or more widely spaced. If it is smaller than or closer together than the average, make it even smaller or closer together.

FRANCIS CONSTRUCTION

Refer to the end of this chapter for more detailed pictures concerning the actual construction of the Francis characters.

This is another version of Francis—same head, but a very different body, and now a different sex. Now she is six heads tall.

And here is still another body shape, but the same head. In this long and lanky form he/she is almost eight heads tall. Which of the pictured bodies is the "right one" for Francis?

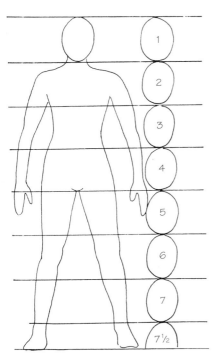

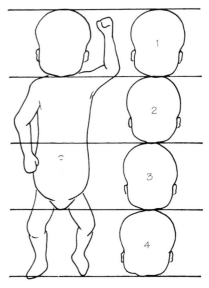

The average adult is approximately seven and one-half heads tall. Use a guideline such as this for determining the length of the legs, arms, neck and torso on your clay creations. Keep in mind it's *only* a guideline. Each figure has its own unique way of being "put together." And you can choose to exaggerate any part or all of them.

Here are the same bodies pictured with the "Francis" head, but now that head is replaced with others from my collection. Compare these characters with the ones with the "Francis" head. Note that now, due to different head sizes, the proportions have changed. The little one is 5 heads tall instead of 4; the middle one is 5.6 heads tall instead of 6, and the largest one is 5.8 heads tall instead of 8.

If you are going to create child figures, pay careful attention to proportions. The proportions of babies are very different from those of adults. Of note is the shortness of their arms and legs. When babies are born they can't touch their hands above their heads, and won't usually be able to do so until around the age of two.

HEAD AS A MEASURE FOR WIDTH

We also must look at the width of the character. Measure the height of your own head and compare it to the width of your shoulders and hips. Measure someone else in your family. Are the proportions the same or different?

According to Jack Hamm in *Drawing the Head and Figure*, the average man is two heads wide at the shoulder, while the average woman is approximately one and three-fourths heads at the shoulder. Men's hips are narrower than their shoulders; the hips of the average woman are about equal to shoulder width. The top of the thigh is approximately the width of the head.

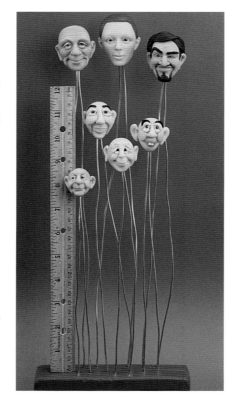

These heads are on wires that make them about eight heads tall, but without sideways dimension to their bodies, they look disproportionately tall. If you were to determine the desired height at this point without actually measuring the head and body, you might clip the wires too short. Then, once the body was filled out with foil, clay or stuffing, it would look shorter than you intended it to be. To be safe, measure using the length of the head as a unit.

MEASURING SHORTCUT

If you don't like rulers and numbers, this measuring stuff can be a bit too much. Is it really necessary? Well, you can always guess. Often that works. But almost as often it doesn't. If your character is seven to nine heads tall, a shortcut formula helps eliminate some measuring. This method divides the body into four equal parts:

1. Top of head to nipples (just below the armpit)
2. Nipples to just above crotch (joint where upper leg bends)
3. Just above crotch to just below knees
4. Just below knees to bottom of foot

Add these general rules (for adults):

1. The elbow is halfway between the armpit and the wrist.
2. The fingertips reach one-third of the distance between the crotch and the bottom of the knee, with the wrist being at the crotch.
3. The distance from the bottom of the chin to the top of the collarbone is one-fourth the length of the head (Redman, *How to Draw Caricatures*).

If you follow these measurements, your character will look quite proportional. Of course, you can always go for charming and whimsical and forget about standards.

If your character is less than seven heads tall, you have to alter the formula. If I make characters with larger-than-average heads, I usually give them a shorter trunk and shorter arms and legs. Refer to the shortest, four-head-tall Francis, at the begin-

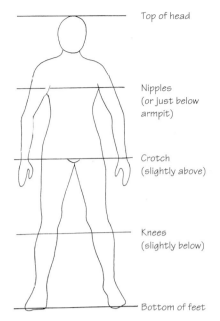

Diagram for dividing the body into four equal parts.

Top of head

Nipples (or just below armpit)

Crotch (slightly above)

Knees (slightly below)

Bottom of feet

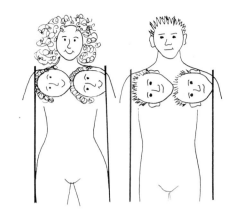

Proportional guideline for the width of the average body.

ning of this chapter. The midpoint of the body is around the navel rather than above the crotch, like it would be on an average adult. These proportions are more like those of a newborn baby. Notice, however, that the wrists still seem to come at about the crotch. A baby's arms are shorter than that.

NOW WHAT?

How do you actually translate this information into a character? I do it one of two ways:

1. Make the head first, and then decide on the character height.
2. Decide on the character height, and then make a head to correspond with it.

If any size character works, I use the first method, since that gives me more freedom. I make a head, mea-

sure it, decide how many heads tall I want the character to be, and then multiply the two numbers together. Thus, a 3" tall head for a seven heads tall character would be a 21" tall finished doll (3 × 7 = 21). And a ½" tall head for a six heads tall character would be a 3" tall finished doll (½ × 6 = 3).

If I am restricted by oven size, cost or already-finished clothing, I use the second method. I determine the height of the finished character, and then divide that number by the number of heads tall it will be. Thus, a 12" character that is six heads tall would have a 2" tall head (12/6 = 2). The trick is to stay true to the predetermined size. The temptation for me is to make a bigger head. The secret is to measure as you work, and cut away clay if the head becomes too big.

Working From Photos

It is not always reliable to work from memory when making a character unless you have fantastic recall or you want to create cartoon-type characters. To create caricatures of real people or to make realistic characters, have good photographs for reference. I keep a book full of them and use them frequently.

These photos of Asha are perfect for sculpting purposes. There are good portrait shots of her face from at least three angles, including a profile. Full-body shots help with proportion and "attitude." Since I don't know Asha, I don't know how to interpret her personality except by what I see in the photos. I also find the three different poses very helpful; they all look natural. Any of them could become the basis for a character or doll.

When using photos, be aware the camera may distort the actual proportions due to the angle of the camera lens. This distortion is known as *foreshortening*, and is a natural process when 3-D images are flattened into 2-D. One way to tell if the image is distorted is to measure something such as the door in the standing photo of Asha. It is wider at the top than at the bottom. This is a distortion of reality, since in real life the sides of the door would be parallel. I can infer from this measurement that Asha's legs would also appear slightly narrower and (I am guessing) shorter than in real life.

Construction Methods for Francis

The rest of the pictures in this chapter show the process I used to complete the "Francis" characters. For more complete instructions on dressing all-clay characters, turn to chapter 6, or refer to my book *How to Make Clay Characters*.

Francis, in the middle, who was pictured at the beginning of this chapter, models with her two other "bodies." She couldn't be in three places at one time, so two of her friends are standing in for her.

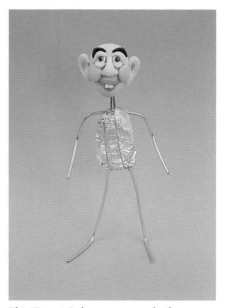

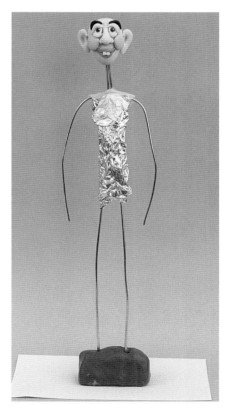

The "Francis" characters were built over an armature made from an inverted *U*-shaped wire (16-gauge fence wire) and aluminum foil. For the arms, a second piece of wire was inserted straight through the foil. Two of the characters have a bent-wire foot, while the third has none. I did this to show two options. It is much easier to put a shoe over straight wire, but the resulting character is not as stable as the one with bent wire. Because clay is somewhat flexible even after baking, the shoe without wire may gradually bend due to the forward weight of the standing character.

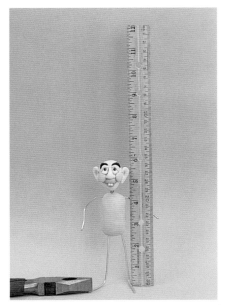 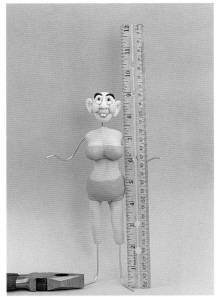 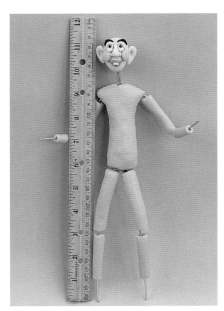

The trunk was then covered with clay. The female version of Francis was embarrassed, so I gave her a bikini! I used a ruler to keep track of how long to make the trunks of each. The midpoint on the body is just above the crotch, or at the bend of the upper leg.

The midpoint is slightly lower on the tall character, since he has long legs. It is higher on the short character, since he has very short legs.

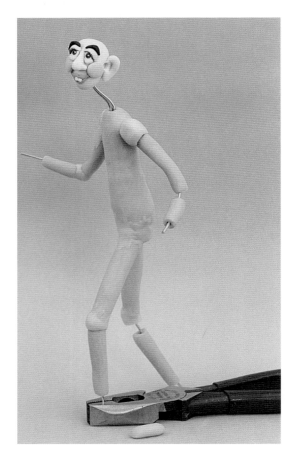

On the tall character I leave gaps at each of the arm and leg joints. After baking, these gaps will allow me to pose him and test out various positions. This is hard to do when the pieces are soft and prone to accidental smashing. Once I am happy with the pose, I fill in the joints with raw clay.

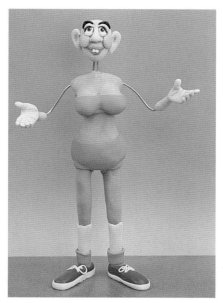
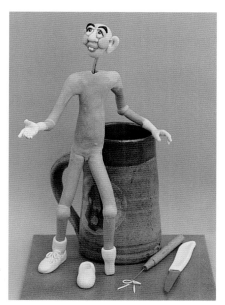

Once the shoes and hands are in place, I bake the characters, propping them as needed.
Large ceramic mugs are ideal for propping tall pieces.

My version of dressing clay characters is to cut out clay pattern pieces very similar to those used for fabric clothing. For finished strength, keep these pieces at least ¹⁄₁₆" thick. Using actual pieces eliminates a lot of sculpting work. Pressing each piece with real fabric will give it a fabric texture. I "sew" the pieces together simply by pressing the seams against each other. The character is then dressed in these clay clothes. (For more instruction on clothing and accessories, turn to the next chapter.)

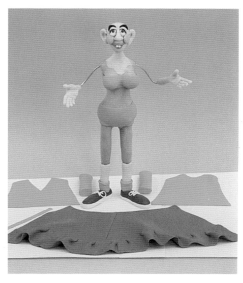

CHAPTER SIX

Simple Cartoon Impressions: Using Accessories

PUTTING IT ALL TOGETHER

You've gathered tools, purchased some polymer clay, and practiced making faces—and they turned out OK! Better than you expected! You might even plan to make caricatures for family, friends and prospective clients. But can you make a person anyone else will recognize?

Take some pressure off yourself. For your first effort at making an actual person, begin with a simple cartoon caricature that captures what you know about a person, not what you see. That way you can concentrate on your clay skills without worrying whether the resulting figure will really look like a specific person. To make it even easier, choose a person who has very recognizable, describable features, such as a beard or a bald head or long braids or overlarge glasses. That way people will say, "Oh, that looks just like so-and-so!" An easy-to-represent occupation or hobby is also helpful.

Once you have chosen a subject, ask some questions to get descriptive information. Though it is helpful to

see a photograph of the subject for coloring and size references, you don't have to have one for this type of caricature, since the actual physical resemblance isn't what's important. In fact, a picture can hinder your work because it may put expectations on both you and the recipient, taking all the joy out of the endeavor. For a first project, you don't need expectations. This is supposed to be fun!

GETTING INFORMATION

I am going to use my brother Matthew for the first example. Follow along by making someone you know. The basic techniques will be the same. Once you see one clay person being built, you will be able to adapt the information to other characters. For instance, removing the hood from Matthew's jacket and changing the jacket's color and texture turns it into a sweater or shirt. If you need more help on how to dress all-clay characters, you might want to refer to my book *How to Make Clay Characters*.

SAMPLE QUESTIONS
1. Name: Matthew
2. Height: 5'8"
3. Build: medium
4. Eye color: blue
5. Hair: light reddish brown, curly at back of neck; mustache and short beard
6. Skin color: fair, Caucasian
7. Eyebrows: curly, low, heavy
8. Work: farmer
9. Hobbies: hunting, fishing
10. Food preferences: Snickers, Mountain Dew, turkey sandwiches
11. Personality: a joker; serious face hides his humor
12. Clothing: blue jeans, John Deere cap, gray button-neck T-shirt with an overshirt, cowboy boots
13. Pose: sitting on a straw bale, holding hunting rifle, a can of Mountain Dew and a fish

When you first practice caricatures, create ones in which the accessories, hair color and clothing give clues to the identity. People who know my brother Matthew know the John Deere hat and sandy beard are dead-give aways. Relying on accessories to make connections eases the stress of getting features exactly right.

MAKE A SIMPLE SKETCH

Once you have some information to work with, draw a simple actual-size sketch of how you "see" the piece in your imagination. It doesn't have to be a good drawing, but it will give you something with which to start. How big will the head be in proportion to the body? Will the legs be long or short? How will the hands and feet be positioned? What direction will the character be looking?

Drawing of Matthew

GENERAL MATERIALS
- pink make-up blush
- round toothpicks
- wire, two 4" pieces, 14-gauge or sturdy coat hanger
- knife
- needle tools, both sharp and blunt
- rolling pin, brayer or pasta machine
- paint, either acrylic or watercolor
- brushes, no. 2 or no. 4 filbert or flat, liner for fine detail
- aluminum foil
- ruler or cutting-and-measuring template for polymer clay
- fabric for texture
- waterless hand cleaner and towel
- sturdy brush handle or 7" piece of ¼" wooden dowel
- wire cutters
- baking pan or ceramic tile
- oven
- oven thermometer
- paper towels

Once you have the concept and the drawing, you can create a specific materials list for your character, including the colors of clay needed.

Step 1: Making the armature. To save on the amount of clay used for the armature and to ensure even and thorough baking, make an aluminum foil armature to put inside the body. Crumple foil and shape it to the approximate size of your drawing. Cover armature with a ⅛" thick layer of clay, adding more in some areas to create the desired body shape. Insert a piece of wire into the neck area. Bake the armature according to directions on the package. Cool.

Step 2: Making pants. Flatten a circle of blue clay large enough to cover the bottom half of the armature. Make two tubes of clay, each as long and as fat at the top as you wish the pant leg to be. Use the paintbrush handle to hollow out the leg to the knee.

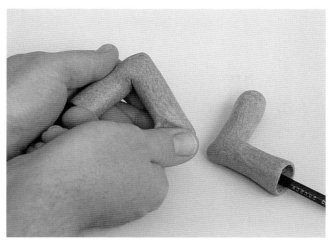

With the brush handle still in the pant leg, bend the leg at the knee. With your thumb, flatten an angled space at the top of each leg.

Press the clay circle over the bottom half of the armature. Trim the waist edge with a knife. Press the pant leg in place; press the pants bottom on top of the angled flat spots.

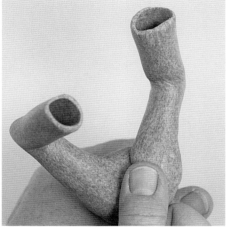

Blend the top leg seam with your thumb to smooth it into the bottom of his pants.

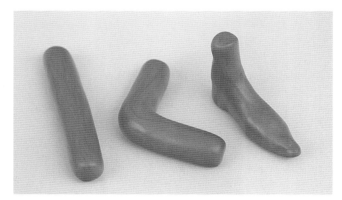

Step 3: Making boots. Determine how tall the boots will be. Roll a rope that tall, plus the length of the foot. The rope should be as thick as the top of the boot. (And the top of the boot should fit into the pantleg.) Bend the rope at the ankle. Shape the boot with your fingers to mimic the pointed toe, instep and heel of a cowboy boot.

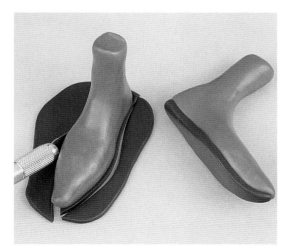

Flatten a piece of darker brown clay to ¹⁄₁₆" thick. Set the boot on top of it and trace the outline of the sole. Use a craft blade to cut out the sole. Smooth the edges. Press to the bottom of the boot.

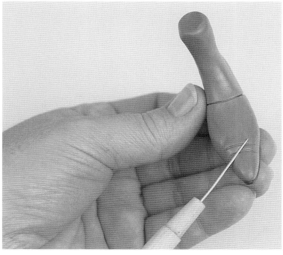

Use a needle tool to press wrinkle lines into the front of the boot.

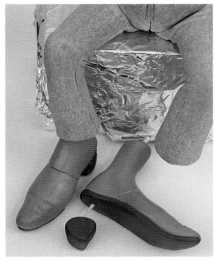

Press a toothpick into the top of each boot, leaving a protruding piece equal to the height of the heel. Form heel with your fingers, making first a ball, and then a heel shape. Press in place over toothpick. Insert boot into pantleg. Bake and cool.

Place head on body. Smooth edges of neck onto body. Press on clay for hair, following hair line. (Note: If this is hard to do without wrecking the face, bake character for 20 minutes to set the face, and then add hair.) Use a needle tool to press in marks to simulate hair.

Sculpt head using directions in chapter 4. Place head on character to determine angle of neck.

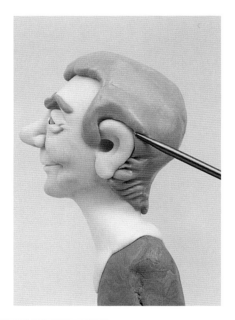

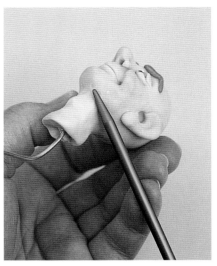

Add clay for neck. Blend edges into head.

Rotate end of needle tool in circles to make curly hair for beard.

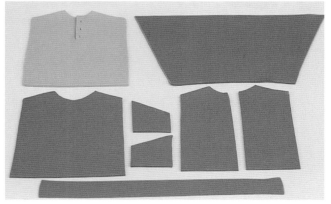

Step 4: Creating the shirt and jacket.
Roll the clay for the shirt and jacket into ¹⁄₁₆" thick sheets. Trace shirt pattern (page 69) pieces onto a sheet of paper, then cut them out. Compare them in size to the clay armature. Modify pieces, making them larger or smaller as needed. (Remember that clay can be stretched somewhat.) For T-shirt, lay pattern on clay and cut out one piece. Cut out jacket pieces. Cut one of jacket pieces in half.

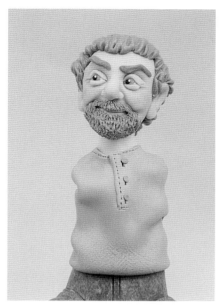

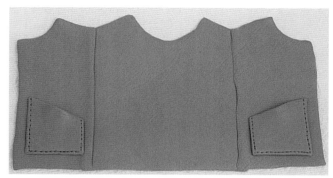

Press jacket side seams together. Press with cloth for texture. Press pockets for texture, and then place them on jacket.

Slit front of T-shirt. Overlap one edge over the other. Draw in stitch marks with a needle tool or wheel. Press on tiny balls for buttons. Lay T-shirt lightly in place on character, marking the waist. Trim shirt slightly longer than waist. Roll under bottom edge and place on character so that rolled edge comes just to waist.

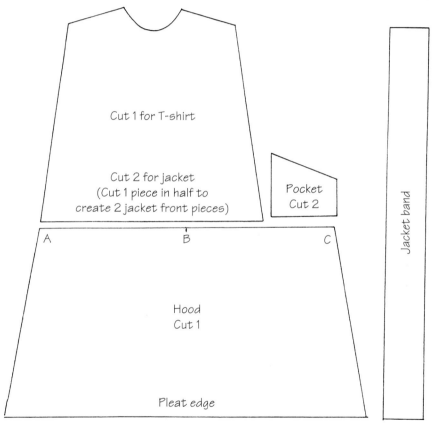

Cut 1 for T-shirt

Cut 2 for jacket
(Cut 1 piece in half to create 2 jacket front pieces)

Pocket
Cut 2

Jacket band

A   B   C

Hood
Cut 1

Pleat edge

Shirt pattern. Enlarge or reduce pattern to fit your specific character. For a longer coat, lengthen pattern at bottom.

Lay jacket band around hips.

Overlap front shoulder piece over back piece. Press excess clay into shoulder area.

Adjust with brush. The soft bristles won't leave harsh marks or fingerprints.

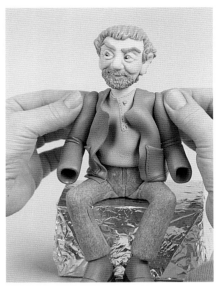

Make shirt sleeves the same shape as the legs, with the sleeve top the width of the upper arm. Taper sleeve slightly toward the wrist. Hollow sleeves to elbows.

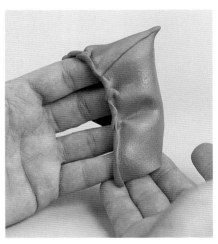

To create hood, fold line AC in half, with B at the hood's peak. Pleat the long edge.

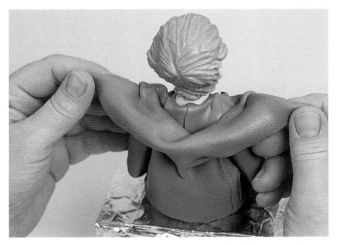

Press hood in place, stretching the ends to make them meet the front edge of the jacket.

Position jacket by lifting and pressing with brush.

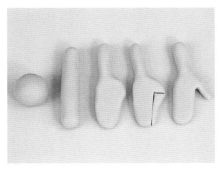

Step 5: Hands.
- Start by rolling two equal balls of clay.
- Roll each into a tube. The thickness of the tube should equal the thickness of the character's lower arm.
- Press the ends into a mitten shape (not too flat!). General rule for adult hands: They're about two-thirds the head length.
- Cut out an area to create the thumb.
- Remove cut out clay.
- Smooth thumb by rolling it between your fingers and patting it into shape.

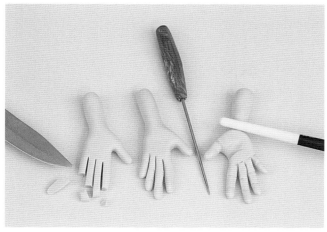

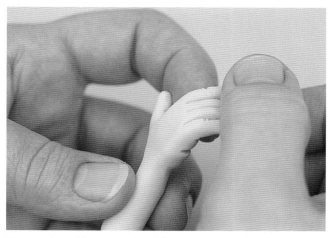

- Cut three lines to create four fingers. Trim to desired length.
- Roll and pat each finger until smooth.
- Use brush handle and needle tool to mark and shape hand.

To create knuckles, gently bend fingers over your hand.

Stroke back of hand, first from back of hand toward fingers, and then from fingers toward back of hand. Stop each stroke at the knuckles. A ridge will form gradually.

Use a needle tool, and then a brush to shape knuckles.

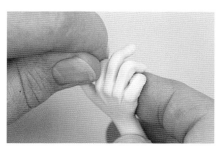

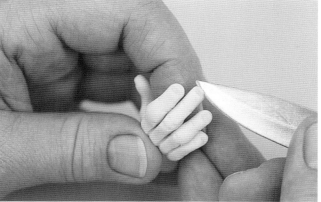

Press in nail marks with a nail tool or the head of a nail or tack. Cut under each nail to create a realistic nail line.

Bend fingers at first joint by bending each over the edge of a knife, and then pinching gently to form a definite bend.

Pose hand as desired. I posed these to hold a soda can and a fishing pole. (When I finished Matthew, I decided that I'd put a clay candy bar into his hand instead of the pole. It worked!)

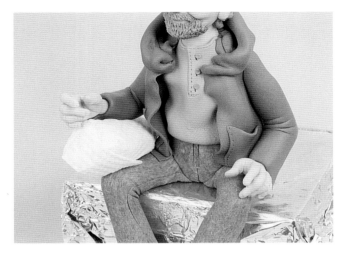

Insert hands into sleeves. Be sure each is at the correct angle to hold an object. Support hands with a wad of paper toweling. (See chapter 9 for other propping ideas.)

Place hat on head (directions for hat are under *Accessories*). Since the hat is already baked, it is rigid and will not lose its shape as you press it in place. Make changes as necessary to make hair look natural around the hat. Bake.

Accessories

Accessories are very important to the life of a character because they give clues to that person's interests and personality. These are just a few of the myriads of things that can be made with polymer clay. For more ideas, check out miniature and dollhouse magazines, plus the book *Making Miniatures in Polymer Clay* by Mary Kalinski.

BAG OF GRAIN

Cut a rectangle shape of desired size. Press clay with fabric to give it baglike texture. Fold rectangle in half. Overlap edges across the bottom, and then up one side, pressing lightly to hold edges together.

OVEN SAFE?

When choosing non-polymer clay accessories to put with your caricatures, keep in mind many things are oven safe at the 265–275°F recommended by most polymer clay manufacturers. This includes wood, glass, ceramic, natural fibers, metal and paper. Some wood will bleed sap at these temperatures, staining the wood and making a mess of your baking pan. If in doubt, test it before putting it into the oven with your character. Or do what I did—I made a replica of the straw bale from foil and cardboard, and then baked Matthew on the fake bale. I replaced it with the real thing for display.

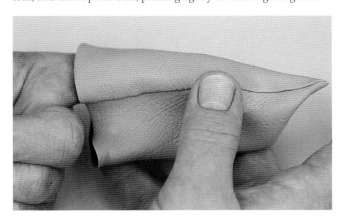

To give the bag form, stuff it with small pieces of paper toweling.

Gather top of bag, and then compress the shape by pressing around the top with a smooth tool.

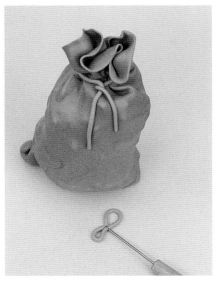

Add a tie, made in two parts as shown.

Bake bags. After baking, paint on a coat of paint, and then wipe it off immediately to leave an antiqued look. Write on the bag with paint or a permanent marker. (Note: Marker lines tend to bleed and blur with age.)

GUN

To make the gun, I used three colors of clay, an empty pen barrel and a black wire bent to look like a trigger. The rigid pen barrel could also become the basic structure for a golf club, a hoe or shovel, a pool cue or a fishing pole. Use your imagination to figure out how to use tiny junk-drawer items as the basis for accessories.

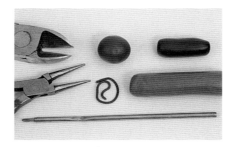

Bake finished gun. Antique for a used or worn look.

SANDWICHES

To make a sandwich, you first need to bake a loaf of clay bread. Cutting a baked loaf, rather than an unbaked clay one, will result in realistic, distinct edges on each slice. To make bread, mix colors until you get the texture and color of your favorite bread (for a whole-wheat look, try adding coarse sand). Bake loaf, and then paint it to get a browned crust. The bread will cut more easily if it is warm, so stick the loaf back in the oven for a few minutes, and then slice.

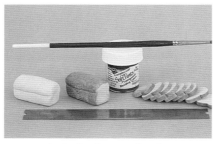

To copy the look of mustard and mayonnaise, paint thick acrylic paint on slices of bread. Make lettuce and meat by mixing transparent polymer clay with color. Press the meat and lettuce very thin, and then rip the edges. Stack on bread; assemble. Bake sandwich; slice in half while still hot.

FISH

For the fish, I used these clay shapes and tools. A change of clay or paint color and an altered shape can easily turn this into a goldfish, a swordfish or a guppy.

After the pieces are assembled, press in scale marks with the edge of a straw or a similar shape.

After baking, antique fish with paint to accentuate the texture, using a transparent paint, acrylic paint or thick watercolor.

HAT

To get a smooth round shape, make a form that mimics the character's head shape. I made this one over aluminum foil. After baking, flatten the hat color to ⅟₁₆" thick. Pat cornstarch on clay to prevent it from sticking to the form.

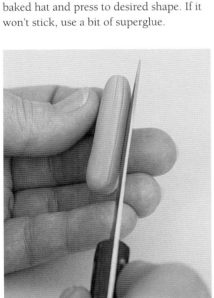

Remove the hat from the form. Shape the bill for the hat. Fit bill to inner edge of baked hat and press to desired shape. If it won't stick, use a bit of superglue.

Bake the hat again. After the hat cools, paint on insignia.

Press the hat clay in place onto the form, trimming edges to make them even. Press on seam marks and emblem. Bake and cool.

CANDY BAR

The candy bar was a last-minute addition. I had originally planned it for the pocket. The candy bar was made by mixing shades of brown clay to simulate the candy bar center, and then wrapping it with a layer of "chocolate" clay. It was baked prior to placing it in Matthew's hand. To simulate the look of bitten candy, I cut it with a dull blade while it was still hot. If you need a translucent appearance to the candy, add translucent clay to the mix.

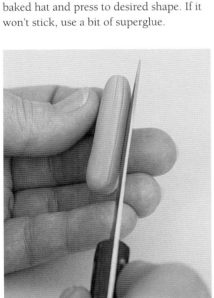

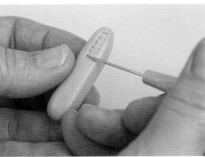

Use a needle tool to make kernel marks.

EARS OF CORN

Form yellow clay into corn shape. Cut in rows of corn.

To shape leaves, roll small balls of clay into teardrop shapes. Flatten them and then stretch them into elongated forms. Press leaves in place, twirling the ends to curl them. Bake the ears. After they are cool, antique with paint, wiping off any excess.

Once all of the parts are baked, assemble the character.

OVERSTUFFED CHAIR

Clay characters are so much more fun if they are part of a setting. One of my favorite accessories is the overstuffed chair. This chair is polymer clay over a cardboard-and-foil armature. The calico pattern is created with millefiori, which is layering clay to create patterns. The pattern is sliced, like refrigerator cookies, and the squares are applied one at a time to the base chair pattern.

This is Rose. A chair of this size (6" × 5" × 4") takes 6 to 8 hours. This one used about twelve ounces of junk clay and twelve ounces of surface clay.

Fold pieces on dotted lines. Fill the seat with firmly crumpled foil to give it support.

Tape chair pieces in place.

Cover the chair with crumpled foil to create its shape. For thick, rounded parts, such as the arm and the top back, roll foil into a tube and then press in place.

Cover the surface with a smooth layer of foil to keep everything in place. Less clay will be needed to cover the chair if the foil is very smooth. Note that the foil was not covered beneath the cushion. A separate piece of cardboard was cut to size to simulate the cushion.

Cover the chair with a layer of junk or left-over polymer clay. It is helpful to look at a real chair to see where the seam lines are in the upholstery pieces. If your clay chair is to look like a new one, keep everything very smooth. If the chair is worn and old, leave it crumpled looking. If you like to work with patterns, copy the shapes of these pieces onto paper so you can use them again for the patterned upholstery.

If you already have a clay character for this chair, see if the chair "fits." It is helpful if the character is already baked so you can press it into the chair to get a realistic look. An unbaked character might distort while pressing it in place.

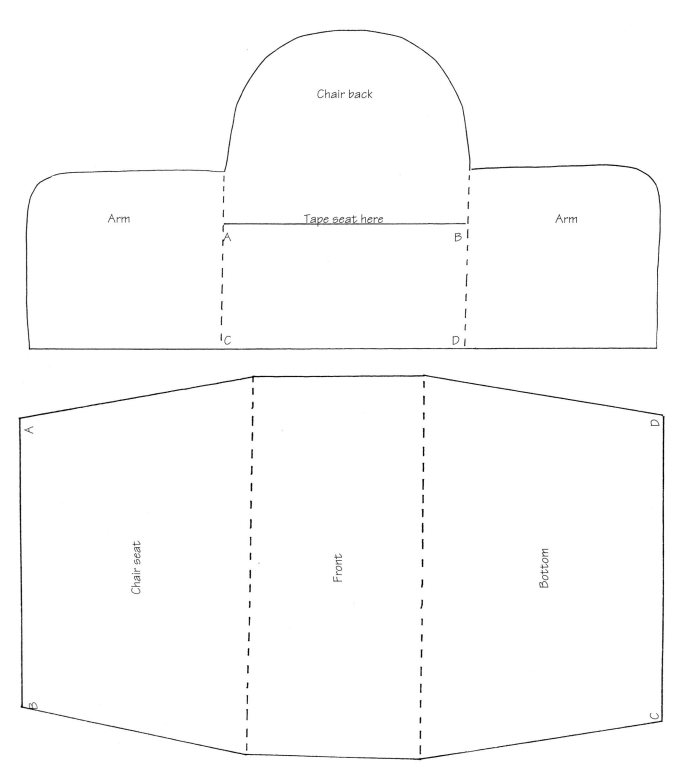

Pattern for chair. Reduce or enlarge the pattern to the size of your choice. Lay the pattern out on cardboard and then cut out pieces. Note that I used a piece of cereal box cardboard.

CREATING THE UPHOLSTERY FABRIC

The process of creating patterned clay, called *millefiori* (meaning *a thousand flowers* in Italian), is endlessly fascinating. For a very special gift, you could actually copy someone's favorite chair. For more help with millefiori, refer to the Resources section.

Decide on the colors and pattern for the chair. A floral print is easy to do and is forgiving, as even mistakes still tend to look like flowers. For a first chair, stay away from patterns that involve matching one piece to another, as in a plaid or a stripe.

WHEN ATTEMPTING MILLEFIORI

When first practicing millefiori, use colors that will be a pleasing mix if you make a mistake and have to wad it all up into a ball and start over. For instance, blue, white and green mixed together would make a pleasing pastel blue-green, but red, green and white would make a muddy brown.

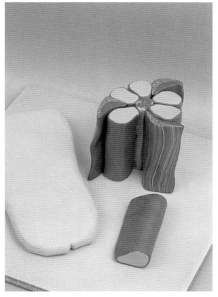

Roll out a rope of flower-colored clay 3" long and 2" thick. Cover this with a clay blanket of contrasting color. Roll rope to one foot long. Cut into six equal pieces for petals. Press each piece into a petal shape. Stand petals around a central rope that will be the flower center. Add green pieces for leaves.

Roll a blanket of clay that will be the background color. Fit this blanket around the flower. Use a blunt needle to press the blanket into the indentations in the flower.

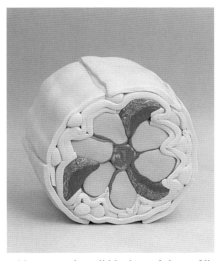

Add ropes and small blankets of clay to fill flower design until it is circular. Try to have air spaces be relatively small: Large air spaces will distort the design.

Squeeze floral rope between your palms to stretch it and reduce its diameter. This will lengthen the rope. Do this slowly so the rope stays circular, uniform and intact. The warmth and pressure of your hands should make it fairly easy to stretch.

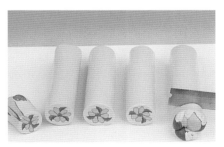

Once the rope is long enough to lay on its side and roll, roll and stretch it until it is 16" long and uniform in diameter. Practice with a piece of plain clay before you try it on the patterned chunk. Trim ends until the end design is clean. Cut into four equal pieces.

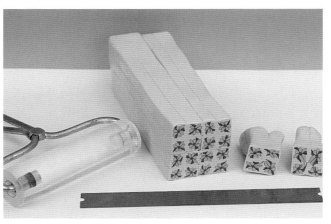

Repeat the rolling and stretching until the piece is 8"–16" long. Keep an eye on the pattern. If it gets to the size that you like for your upholstery fabric, stop rolling!

Roll each piece with a brayer until the sides are slightly square, and then stack them into a cube. Roll each side and then stretch the cube. Repeat this until the rope is again 16" long. Trim ends and cut into four equal pieces.

Since I wanted a tiny calico print, I repeated the process to create 64 flowers in each slice. This picture shows the progression of the process. We started with 1 flower, then 4, then 16, then 64. I stacked the pieces a fifth time so I would have a larger chunk from which to make my slices for the chair.

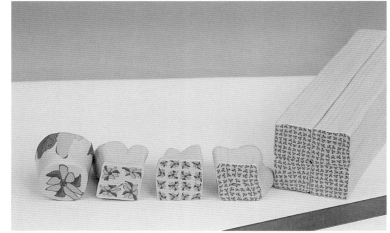

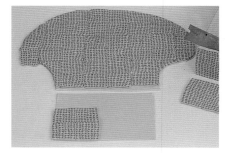

To upholster the chair, cut basic shapes from a sheet of junk clay that is close to the color of the floral background. That way, if a hole shows through the pattern, it won't be so obvious. Slice the millefiori loaf as thinly as possible and apply the pieces to the pattern pieces. Press the surface with a brayer or your palms to "erase" the seam lines and even out the "fabric." Try not to stretch the pieces since it will distort the design.

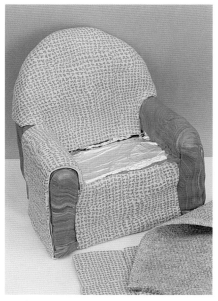

Fit the pieces onto the chair, stretching or trimming them to fit.

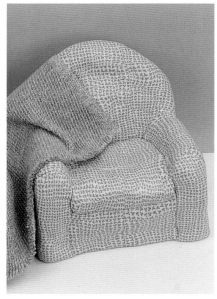

Press the chair with fabric to create a texture similar to real upholstery fabric. Bake.

This chair could be a caricature even though there is no person in sight. It could be a portrait of someone's favorite chair. Can't you imagine the person who was just sitting in this chair? Everything visible in this picture is patterned polymer clay—no paint!

This sitting bench is a variation of the chair pattern. The cardboard armature was stuffed with small stones for added weight. The bench, made from gold Premo! Sculpey, was distressed with a needle tool to simulate the look of wood. After baking, it was antiqued. Another reason this piece is included here is because I wanted to show the effectiveness of two characters who relate to each other. Be careful to get their eyes in the right position if you wish them to interact ("No Need for Words," FIMO and Premo! Sculpey; bench is 10" × 6" × 5").

FLOWERS

These flowers were created for the AnaBel sculpture in chapter 7. It is easy to make variations of these flowers to match specific preferences. For more help with making flowers, refer to *Making Miniature Flowers With Polymer Clay* by Barbara Quast.

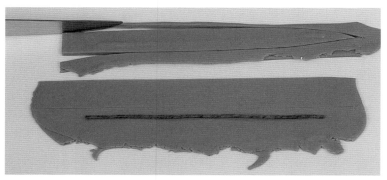

Step 1. For strength and support, there is a wire centered in each of the leaves and flower stems. To help the wires bond to the clay, coat each with white glue. (I used SOBO.) Let dry. For lily leaves, lay wire on a sheet of flattened clay. Cover with a second piece of clay and cut out the leaf shape. Press edges between your fingers to slightly ruffle them. For stems, center a wire through a short rope of clay. Roll and stretch the rope until it is at least the length of the wire and of desired thickness. Trim the ends.

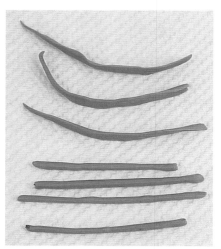

Step 2. Lay leaves and stems on a sheet of paper toweling and then bake.

Step 3. Press a small piece of green clay to flower stem end. Make six petal shapes by flattening small balls of clay and then stretching each into a lily petal. Press three petals to raw green clay at top of stem. Add three more petals in between the first three. Curl the ends. Use a blunt needle tool to hollow out center of the flower, making sure the wire is close enough to the top of the flower to support it.

Step 4. Place flowers in a stand made from crumpled aluminum foil. Bake flowers thoroughly. Since they are so thin and fragile, be sure they are strong.

Step 5. Tint flowers with acrylic paints or transparent paints.

CHAPTER SEVEN

Almost "Real" Caricatures: Capturing a Likeness

Let's talk about sculpting a face that really resembles an actual person. Sculpting caricatures of real people is nearly the same as sculpting generic characters. Everything you've learned so far about sculpting faces will apply in this chapter. What's different is that in order to capture a likeness, you have to pay attention to details.

I know—that sounds too simple. Aren't we always paying attention to the details? Didn't we measure and trim and push and pull and add and smooth, way too many times to count, on each character in this book? True, but in order to make caricatures that capture a likeness, we have to pay attention to size, shape and the relationship between all of the parts. All of the time. On each feature of the face. Otherwise the caricature will not look like the person that it is intended to be.

In chapter 3 I listed questions to ask when looking at the shapes that make up a face. I'll repeat them here because they are important to remember as we sculpt with specific results in mind.

1. What is the shape?
2. Where does it start?
3. What direction does it go?
4. Where does it stop?
5. How does it relate to the features around it?

To do caricatures you also need to ask how the subject's face relates to an average face. Read chapters 2 and 3 again if these points seem unclear.

Wilbert and Milton have many things in common, but their body proportions are definitely not one of those things. Wilbert, on the left, has larger-than-average hands, feet and head. This makes him look whimsical and cartoonish. Milton has very average proportions, which make him look more like a real person.

SCULPTING FOR SPECIFIC RESULTS

Follow along as I make Milton. My intent is to create a face with average, not exaggerated, features. I continually check the shape and size of his features to see if they fit the face I have in mind. Though he is not a caricature of an actual person, the questions I ask and the process I go through while sculpting him are the same as when I capture an actual likeness.

Note: When I made Milton I was

This is Milton, Mr. Average Guy.

trying to make a realistic face, so I did not exaggerate the features. You may wish to make a more whimsical caricature with overlarge or diminutive features. The following demonstration still applies. The questions and the process are valid whether your style is whimsical or realistic. In order for the caricature to capture a likeness, you still have to pay close attention to (a) the shape of the features and (b) the relationship or spacing between features. A general rule for caricature is: If a shape or space is larger or farther apart than average, make it even larger, and vice versa. To do this you must know what average is while staying true to the basic shape of the subject's features.

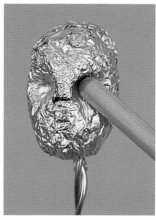
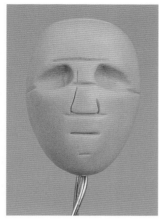
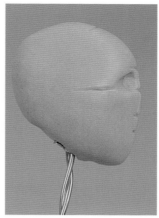
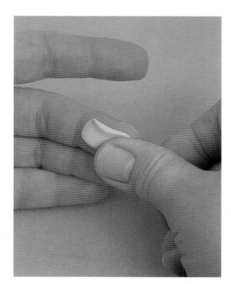

The likeness starts with the armature. What shape is the head? Round? Square? Long? Look at the head from all angles. Where are the eyes in relation to the rest of the head? How far apart are they? How close are they to the sides of the head? The answers to these questions will determine the shape of the foil and placement of the eye sockets. Don't hurry at this stage. The armature may never show, but its effect on the clay does.

Cover the armature with clay. Draw in the features. Now is the time to determine the relationship of the parts, both to each other and to an average face. Is the mouth high or low? Is the nose broad or narrow? Do you want to exaggerate some parts? Make adjustments as needed. It's easier to do it now, before the clay features are in place.

Check the profile. How does it compare with your subject's profile? Draw a straight line from forehead to chin. What angle is the line? What facial features are behind the line? What parts are in front of it? Build up the forehead and chin as needed.

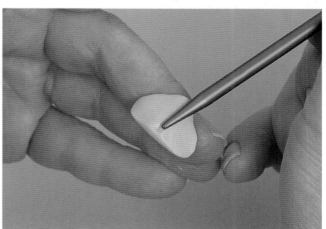

Shape lips, both lower and upper. How thick are your subject's lips in relation to their width? The lips can still be changed after they are added to the face, but this step gives you a head start.

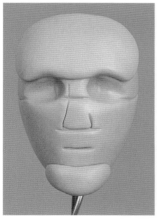
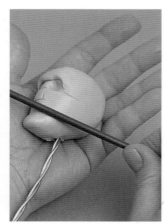

Check the shape of the face from the front. Do the width and length still look like those of your subject's face? Still OK?

Blend in the added clay.

Place lips over the mouth line. How far should the corners extend? Judge where the pupils will be, and compare width of mouth with pupils. (Note: On small faces I don't add the eyes until after the cheeks are in place, as it seems hard to blend without interfering with the eyes. On faces larger than 3" tall, it may be easier to add the eyes in the beginning.) Trim lip pieces at nose line and just above chin. Stay true to your first sketch lines.

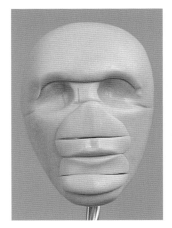

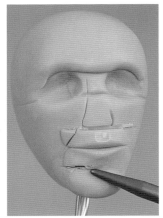

Blend and smooth edges. Don't make it "perfect" at this point. Just rough it in.

Use a blunt tool to roll down across lips and cheeks to broaden and shape them.

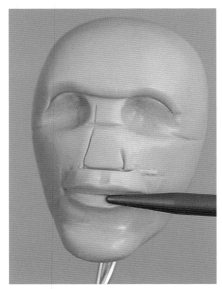

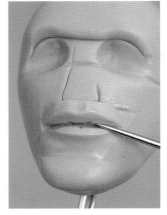

Define the shape of the lips. Check the line between your subject's lips. Is it symmetrical or asymmetrical?

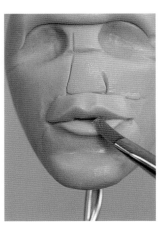

Smooth and shape lips with a clay brush.

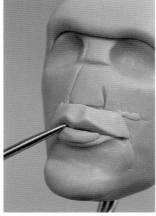

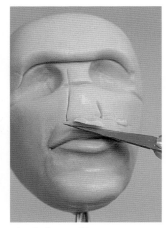

Check the shape of the lips with your picture or model. Too full? Too thin? Turn your sculpture to compare it from all angles. I decide to add a piece to Milton's lower lip to make it fuller.

Check the profile again. Now the upper lip seems to protrude more than I intended, so I trim some away.

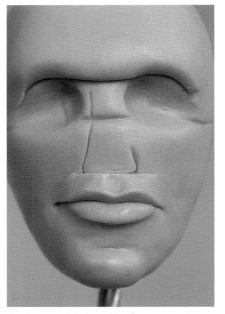

I'm happy with these lips for now, so I leave them and go on to the nose.

Shape the nose and put it in place. Check with your picture or model. Where does the model's nose start in comparison with the eyes? What shape is it? What is the angle of slant? How close is it to the lips? How wide is it? Do you want to exaggerate any part of it?

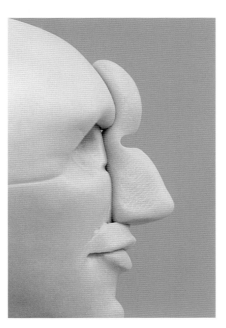

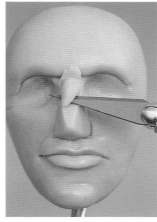

Here I see the top of the nose protrudes more than I want, so I carve some away.

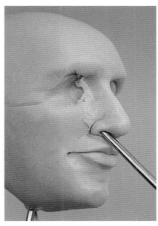

Add nostrils and check shape again.

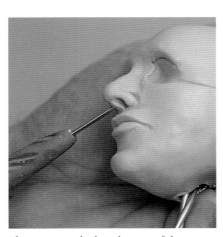

The septum, which is the part of the nose that is between the nostrils, slopes up more than that of my mental image, so I add some clay.

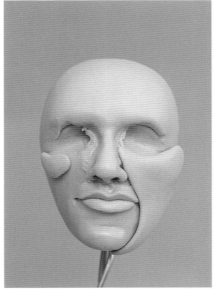

Determine the shape of the cheeks. The cheekbone was not prominent enough on the foil armature, so I add a pad for a cheekbone. How much flesh is on the face of your model? I add a clay shape that mimics the flesh of the cheek. This shape extends around the face and toward the ear: It is not just on the front of the face.

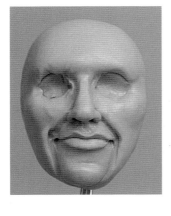

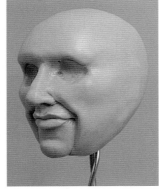

Blend the cheeks into the nose and the sides of the face. Does your subject have deep crease lines between the mouth and cheeks? If you want the caricature to be smiling, be sure your subject smiles so you can see what happens to the lines around the mouth. In a profile view, when the subject smiles, does the corner of the mouth still show, or is it hidden by the curve of the cheek?

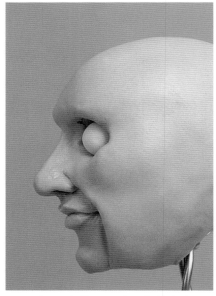

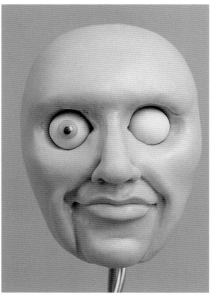

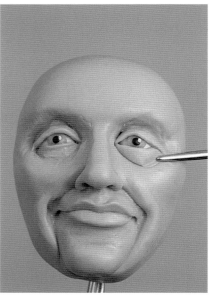

Insert the eyeballs. I used prebaked white clay eyeballs. On your model, how deep are the eyes? How much of the bridge of the nose still shows in a profile view?

Check the eyes from the front. Check the spacing in comparison with your subject's. Are the eyes larger or smaller than your subject's? Is that how you want them to be? Note: I put colored clay irises and pupils on Milton as I didn't want him to have a blank look in the rest of the pictures. You could choose to leave the eyes white and paint them after baking.

Add eyelids. Blend. What is the slant of the eyelids? How much of the upper lid shows? How big are the bags under the eyes? What is the shape of the lower lid?

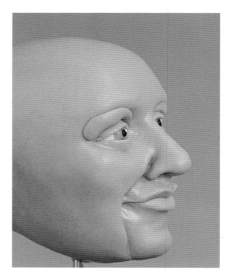

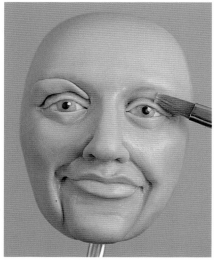

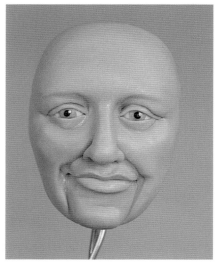

Add clay to the area between the eyebrow and eyes as needed.

Blend and smooth the face.

Check the face from all angles. Do the shapes match those of your subject? Does everything work together? When I step back and look at the total face, I don't think these lips work for this character. Now is the time when I wish I had a model or picture in front of me! Working from just an image in my mind gives mismatched results. I also think that unconscious images are working their way into the sculpture.

I give in to my intuition about the lips and change the shape. I also fill in some of the crease lines between the nose and chin. The face sits more easy with me now. When you first start sculpting, making changes like this may be hard to do since you might not want to destroy something you've worked so hard on. But don't be afraid to make alterations. What good is it if the lips look sensitive or expressive if they aren't the right lips for that character?

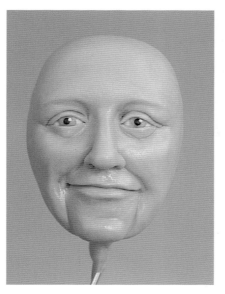

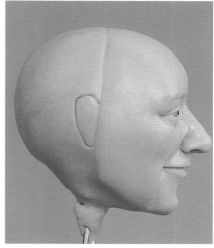

Check the profile again. Draw in the placement of the ear.

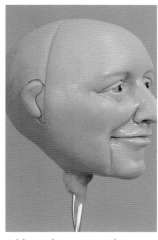

Add a pad to support the ear.

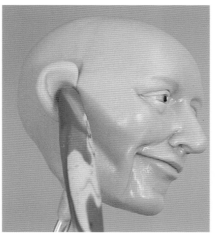

Press a *C*-shaped ear in place.

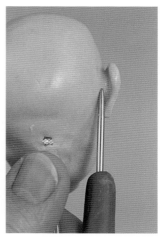

Blend the back of the ear into the head.

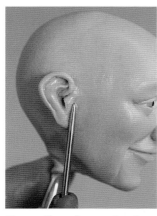

Use needle tools to sculpt the ear. Is it angled in the same direction as your subject's ear? Is the lobe the shape of your subject's earlobe?

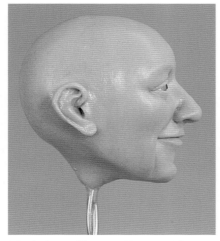

Check the profile again. Do you wish to make any changes? It's not too late!

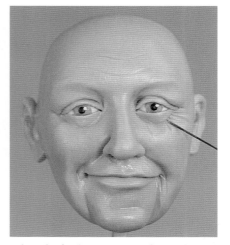

When the final smoothing is finished, create wrinkle lines. To make wrinkles subtle, smooth and blend them with a brush and a light coat of waterless hand cleaner.

Add clay eyebrows if desired.
Be careful of the shape. Really
look at the eyebrows of your
model. Where do they start?
Where do they stop? Where is
the highest point of each? Look
at the neck and determine the
angle.

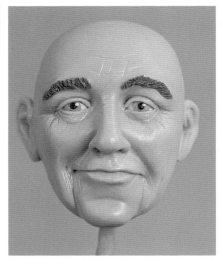

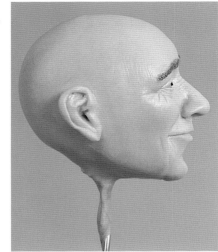

Make a hollow neck of the desired size. Blend neck into
head.

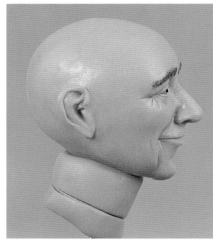

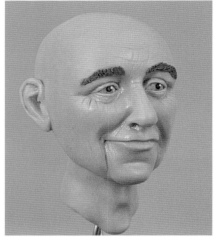

Check final results. Bake the head.

Whoops! Have I ever said that
it's not done until it's baked?
Well, maybe the truth is that it
is never done until we say so!
And for perfectionists like me,
saying "Finished!" is a very
hard thing to do. After baking
Milton, it just seemed that his
eyes were without expression,
blank. So… I took a knife and
carefully removed the clay irises and pupils and …

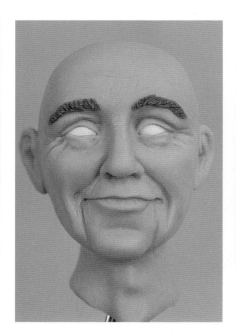

… painted them when I painted and finished the rest of his head. *Now* I am done!

Caricatures of Family and Friends

AUNT NELLIE

It was a great pleasure for me to sculpt this caricature of my Aunt Nellie. She has such a good-humored twinkle. The key to capturing her image was the spacing between her mouth and nose, the shape of her eyes, her hair and her glasses. I sculpted her on an upside-down *U*-shaped wire-and-foil armature. There is no wire in the arms.

Pictures of my Aunt Nellie.

COUSIN ELAINE

You saw this sculpture earlier, but I wanted to show it in connection with photos of Elaine. This is a caricature that didn't quite work. (None of my family recognizes her! That should make you feel good, Elaine!) But I like it so much I decided to include it here. I exaggerated her chin, which I think works, but her mouth isn't quite right and the eyes are too wide open. What I especially like is the way I used purchased polymer clay millefiori designs to capture her T-shirt. It was made very much like a combination of Matthew's shirt and jacket in chapter 6. I pressed on the millefiori designs while the pieces were still flat on the table.

Pictures of my cousin Elaine.

 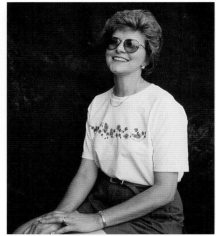 

UNCLE WAYNE

Uncle Wayne's caricature was one of the easiest to do. Once I got the shape of his head and the spacing of his features, I had him. Uncle Wayne has always been a tease. I hope that he enjoys this gentle teasing on my part!

Pictures of Uncle Wayne.

ANABEL

I've been making caricatures of my mother AnaBel off and on for thirty years. If I remember right, the first one that I made didn't stay visible in her living room very long! I hope she likes this one better. She has a wonderfully expressive smile and mischievous eyes, so once I got the expression right, I felt that it *was* her.

Construction note. I baked the piece sitting on the flower pot to portray Mom's interest in flowers. Directions for making the flowers are in chapter 6. Note in the unbaked piece how her hands are positioned for the flowers, which will be added after everything is baked. The finished sculpture was dry-brushed with acrylic paint to give more dimension to the clothing colors. For more pictures and another sculpture of AnaBel, refer to the last character in chapter 8.

CHAPTER EIGHT

Turning Caricatures Into Dolls: Four Easy Doll Shapes

MAKING DOLLS

Clay caricatures needn't be limited to all-clay figurines; they can be dolls as well. To me this means they have cloth clothes rather than clay ones. Otherwise, figurines and dolls are much alike. Making clay caricatures into dolls is especially appropriate if you like to sculpt heads larger than 2" in height. Most home ovens won't accommodate figures that are larger than 10" tall, so these larger heads, unless you make them into busts, will be best if made into dolls. In this case, making dolls is not only a fun alternative, it is practical as well.

The principles of proportion are the same whether you are creating a clay figure or a doll, and so are the basic sculpting techniques. So what you learned in the first seven chapters of this book is applicable to doll-making and figure-making. What is different is the armature and the body construction. When making dolls, you do not have rigid clay to give strength and substance to the body like you do with figures. Be sure the armature and/or body shape will provide the desired form plus strength and durability.

There are many ways to give form plus strength to a doll. To get you started, I chose four of my personal favorites. Each has a distinct look and function, and each basic idea yields many variations.

MATERIALS

- sewing machine
- sewing needles and long doll-making needles
- thread
- an assortment of fabrics
- fiberfill (except for puppet)
- wire cutters, both heavy duty and small
- 14- and 24-gauge wire (except for puppet)
- hemostat for stuffing
- glue (a cyanoacrylate glue, such as Pic Stic or Zap A Gap, and a heavier glue such as FabriTac)
- duct tape (except for puppet)

SEWING PATTERNS

You will notice I do not give specific patterns or sewing instructions for clothing. Pattern-making for clothes is beyond the scope of this book. Also, each of your caricatures should be dressed in clothing custom-sized and appropriate for that specific person. A book on clothing that's very helpful to me is *The Doll's Dressmaker* by Venus Dodge.

Bolster Doll

I call this the bolster doll because the base looks like the bolster that was on my grandmother's couch. I particularly like this doll because it is simple, yet almost animated. You can pose this doll in countless ways.

Its body construction can also double as clothing, so there is minimal sewing. Because this doll is not dressed in realistic clothing, you can choose fibers and patterns that tell us things about its "owner." For instance, we can tell that Shandella likes quilting and embellishment and that she has a dramatic flair. The pattern on Shandella's clothing might look out of scale if it were used on made-to-be-real clothing, but for this bolster-style doll, I think it works.

I have done other dolls like this with multiple pockets into which I have stuffed things that are meaningful to that person, such as feathers, cartoon clippings, seed packages, letters and beads. This pattern would be particularly appropriate for a Father Christmas doll, with his long, flowing robes covering up the bolster effect of the base.

ADDITIONAL MATERIALS

- finished doll head sculpted on doubled wire; the doubled wire should measure at least two-thirds the length of the body; I used 14-gauge fence wire and an aluminum foil core for Shandella.
- finished doll hands sculpted on a wire; wire length should equal twice the arm length; I used 14-gauge fence wire wrapped on the end with floral tape. (Instructions are on page 100.)
- cardboard circle equal to diameter of doll base
- plastic pellets, sand or grain for weighting doll

Do you recognize these dolls? You first met Shandella in chapter 3. Annie, whom we first called the Freckle-Faced Girl, was in chapter 4. (Mostly FIMO with Mix Quick; 17½" and 15" tall; Shandella's hair is black CURLY HAIR polypropylene filament; clay applique eyes and eyebrows, painted lips and cheeks; Annie's hair is Curly Craft 100% natural curled fibers; painted face.)

MAKING THE DRESS

Sew dress in the following order:

1. Cut out pattern pieces.
2. Sew back seam to large dot. All seams are ¼". Sew shoulder seams and the top arm seams. Press seams.
3. Add trim to dress if desired.
4. Sew facing shoulder seams. Fit right side of facing to right side of dress at neckline, matching small dots. Sew in place. Clip curves to seam line. Turn facing to inside. Press.
5. Sew side and underarm seams. Clip underarm seam.
6. With right sides together, pin base circle to bottom of dress, easing to fit. Sew in place. Turn dress.

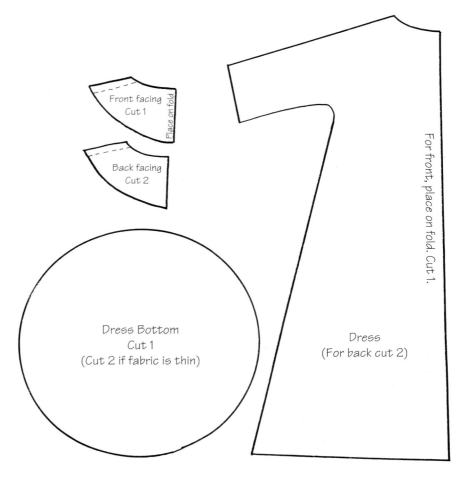

Pattern pieces for bolster doll.

DRESS MAKING CALCULATIONS

Select fabric that fits the personality of your doll. Enlarge pattern pieces to appropriate size. To determine this, decide how tall you want the finished doll to be. For example, I decided to make Shandella seven heads tall. Then I made the following calculations:

- (head length) × (number of heads tall) = total height
  (2½") × (7") = 17½"
  height of doll = 17½ inches
- (height of doll) – (head length) – (neck length) = dress length
  (17½") – (2½") = 15", then (15") – (½") = 14½"
  dress length = 14½ inches

ASSEMBLING THE BOLSTER DOLL

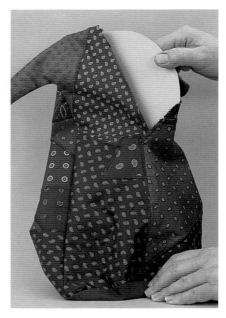

Place cardboard circle in bottom of dress.

Wrap ends of wire with duct tape. This will prevent them from inadvertently poking through the sides of the doll's body. To hold tape and wires in place, twist a length of smaller wire firmly around the tape. This doll is poseable and, over time, it may be bent and repositioned many times. You don't want it to fall apart internally, with no way to fix it except to take the doll apart, so make those wires secure!

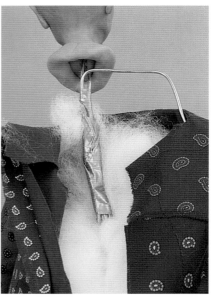

To give weight to doll, fill the bottom of the dress to a depth of 2½" with plastic pellets, grain or sand.

Stuff body partially full with fiberfill so it will support the head. Insert head into body. Place arm into sleeve. Determine placement of shoulder. Bend arm wire at that point. Bend wire again so it runs alongside neck wire.

Tape arm wire to neck wire.

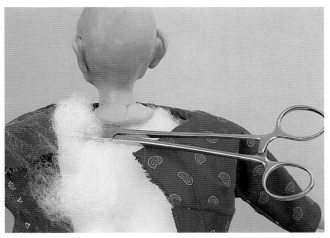

Fill body firmly with fiberfill, using hemostats (if you have them) to place stuffing into the arms.

Repeat with second arm. Wrap a small wire over all three larger wires, twisting the ends to secure the small wire.

Sew back opening almost to top, and then continue stuffing.

When doll is firmly stuffed, finish sewing back opening so that dress fits securely around neck.

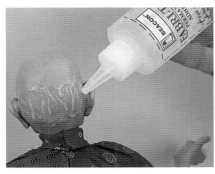

To glue on hair, add heavy glue to one section of head at a time, starting in the back.

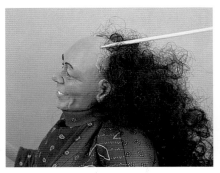

Immediately press on hair in direction that it would normally grow. Use a damp stick to position hair, as the glue will not stick to damp wood.

Continue gluing hair to the sides and then the top. Arrange hair as desired.

WIRE-LOOP HANDS

The techniques used in chapter 6 for making hands are adequate for dolls that sit on a shelf and are never touched again (except for dusting). But once you get into making larger dolls that are actually played with, you will need an armature in the hands for strength and support. The simplest armature is the wire loop. This doesn't add any strength to the fingers, but it does allow you to strengthen and position the wrist.

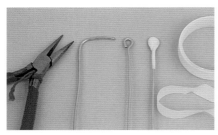

Cut a wire twice the arm length. On one end of wire, measure a distance equal to the desired hand length. At that point, bend the wire at a right angle. Use pliers to bend the end of wire into a loop. Cover the loop with two layers of floral tape.

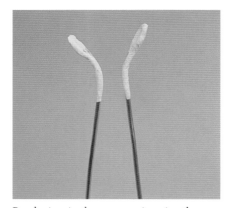

Bend wires in the way you imagine the doll's wrists to bend.

NOTE
Occasionally during the baking process the wax from the floral tape melts and runs onto the surface of the hand. Once the wax is cooled, it does not seem to cause any lasting problems, but it will look scary when you first see it.

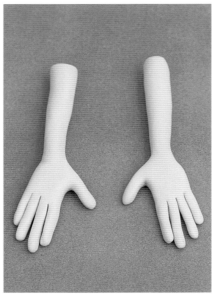

Make hands to fit size of doll, using the instructions in chapter 6. (The average hand is about three-fourths the length of the face.)

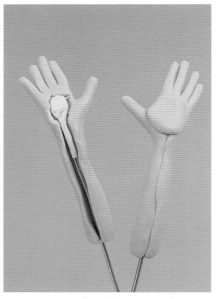

Insert wires into hand. Close arm clay around wire. Add a pad of clay to palm.

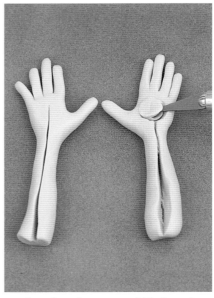

On the palm side, use a craft blade to slit arm and to remove shallow circle from the center of the palm.

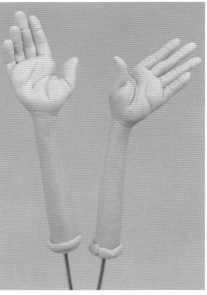

Smooth and blend clay. Finish hands using tips in chapter 6. The ring around the top of each arm aids in attaching the clothing to the arm.

BOLSTER DOLL VARIATION

Annie is a free spirit who is fond of romantic period costumes and gatherings such as the Renaissance Festival.

Assemble Annie the same as you did for Shandella.

Sew a running stitch once around the waist and once slightly above the waist.

Make a belt, vest or corset to cover stitch lines.

Finish doll by adding a necklace (in this case also made of polymer clay), hair and a headpiece in a style of your choice.

Pull threads tight to cinch and form waist.

Button-Joint Doll

A button-joint doll can be a play doll for grownups. Wilbert is sitting on the computer as I write this, and he is definitely trying to get in his two cents worth! This doll invites interaction.

Like the bolster doll, the body structure can become the clothing, so those who don't like to sew clothing may find this pattern appealing. This pattern is also versatile.

You first met Wilbert in chapter 4. Do you recognize him with his hair? (Mixed polymer clay with clay applique eyes and eyebrows; painted lips and eyelashes; hair is unprocessed wool; seated doll is 8¼" tall)

ADDITIONAL MATERIALS

- finished doll head sculpted on a doubled wire; doubled wire length should measure at least two-thirds of the body length; I used 14-gauge fence wire and an aluminum foil core
- finished doll hands; I used hands sculpted over an outline wire (instructions on page 103.)
- finished doll feet (instructions on page 106.)
- plastic pellets, sand or grain for weighting doll

ASSEMBLY

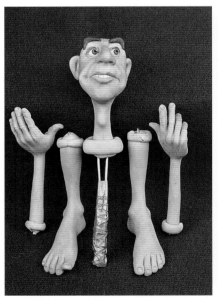

To aid in doll assembly, sculpt head, hands and feet with a clay ring at the top of each piece. Don't make the ring too thick or it won't fit into cloth arm and leg pieces. Wrap head wires with duct tape and wire just like you did for the bolster doll.

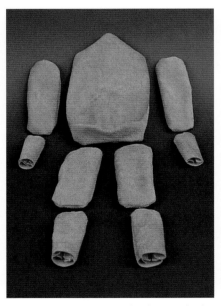

Follow instructions to make the nine body pieces.

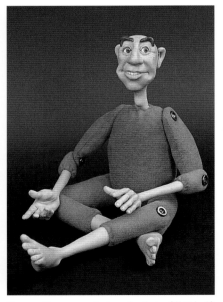

Pour pellets or grain into body to fill it half full. Add head. Fill with fiberfill, and then gather opening around neck. Lightly stuff each arm and leg. Insert clay pieces, and then gather fabric to close openings. Sew arms in place. Sew through the buttons at each joint to make joints more mobile. Notice at the elbows there is a button on the back and front of the joint.

To give more fluid action to the knee joint, attach the lower part of the leg to one edge of the upper leg, as in the picture. Sew upper legs in place using one button on each side. To make his body "clothing" seem more finished, I added a cuff to both his pants and shirt. This was hand sewn in place.

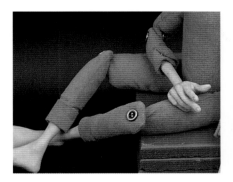

WIRE-OUTLINE HANDS

Sometimes in order to give the right expression to your dolls, you will need to make hands that have support in each finger. There are several different ways to build armatures for hands. The following is a simplified version of a method taught to me by dollmaker Diane Keeler, which I call *wire-outline hands*.

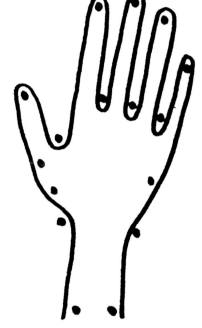

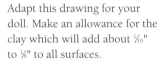

Adapt this drawing for your doll. Make an allowance for the clay which will add about $\frac{1}{16}$" to $\frac{1}{8}$" to all surfaces.

Place the drawing on a piece of wood and pound in nails to mark the outline.

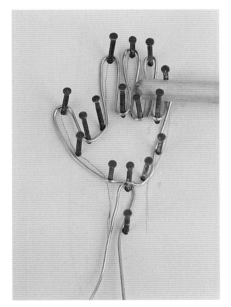

Wrap wire around the outline, using a tool to press the wire in place. The wire in the picture is 18-gauge copper.

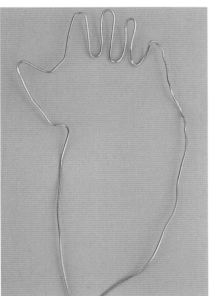

Loosen the outline and remove it from the form. This will distort it, but you will still see where the bends are placed.

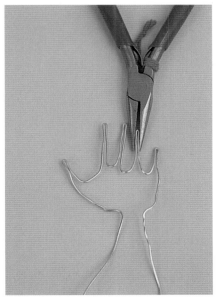

Use pliers to tighten the curve of each fingertip.

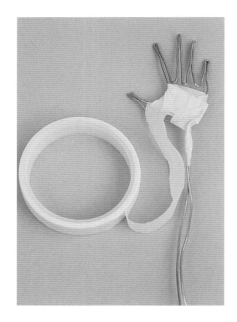

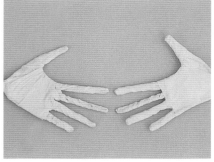

Wrap hands with floral tape, stretching the tape as you wrap to keep the surface smooth.

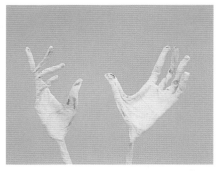

Use pliers to put appropriate bends at finger joints. Position hands.

Pattern pieces for button-joint doll. Alter or enlarge basic pattern as needed to fit your character.

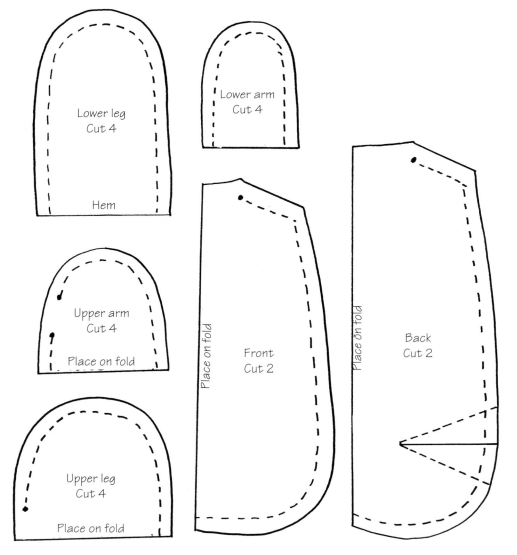

Lower leg
Cut 4

Hem

Lower arm
Cut 4

Upper arm
Cut 4

Place on fold

Place on fold

Front
Cut 2

Place on fold

Back
Cut 2

Upper leg
Cut 4

Place on fold

Add a pad of clay to both the palm and the back side of the hand. Notice that the pad on the palm is thicker at the thumb side.

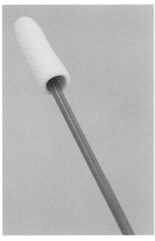

Hollow a clay tube to place on each finger.

Press all pieces in place.

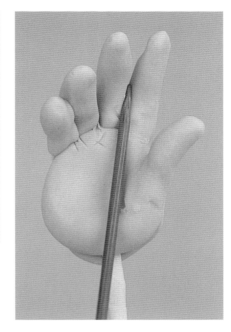

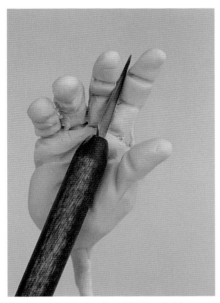

Carve away excess clay. Mark wrinkle lines. Be sure that clay is pressed firmly to the wire armature and that it is not loose or full of air. This may require pinching the clay and temporarily distorting the shape. You may also find that you will need to stretch and trim the fingers to make them thin enough.

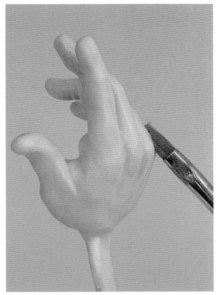

Do the final smoothing and shaping with the clay brush.

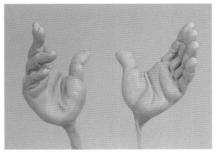

Check overall shape of hands.

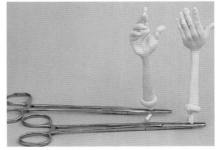

Add clay for the arm. Wilbert has very skinny arms and legs, which I made even more so in his caricature. Hemostats work very well for supporting the hands in an upright position: They can even go in the oven!

BARE FEET

Determine the size of the feet. Roll a tube of clay the diameter of the leg. Bend it to create the needed foot length. Pull out the heel to make it protrude.

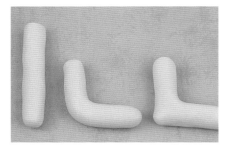

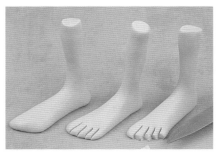

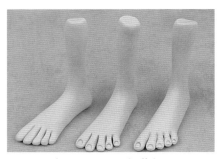

Flatten the foot so that it slopes downhill like a mini ski slope. Don't let it wrinkle at the ankle. Cut in four lines to create five toes. Trim toe lengths.

Use your fingers to round off the toes. Add toenails and lines, the same as for hands, only there is only one joint on each toe, not two as on fingers.

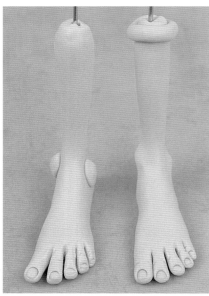

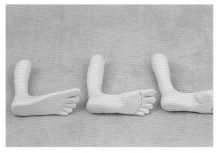

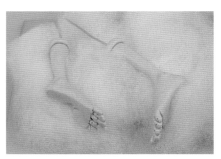

Press your thumb against the big-toe side of the foot to create an arch. Add lines to the bottom of the foot. Soften them with the clay brush.

Bake feet on a bed of fiberfill to prevent the bottom side from getting flat. (Caution: Be sure that there is adequate circulation in the oven and that the bottom of the pan is not close to the heating element in the oven.)

Add small balls of clay for the ankle bones. Check out your own to see where they are placed. Blend. Add a ring at the top of each leg.

BUTTON-JOINT DOLL VARIATIONS

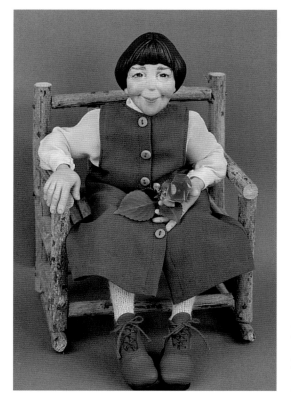

Here's Lu again, whom you first met in chapter 3. This time I made her into a doll (which, of course, she always has been!). At first glance it doesn't seem that she is related to the button-joint doll, but let's look again.

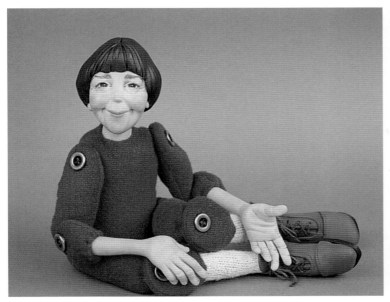

Sure enough, Lu has on a body suit very similar to Wilbert's. However, this outfit did not really fit Lu's personality, so I made her an outfit that was more classic. I couldn't do anything about those wool socks and oversized shoes, though, so they had to stay as part of her ensemble. Sometimes still, despite careful planning, the size of things gets away from me!

I have been making dolls for many years now, and I am still surprised and delighted when I finish a doll and witness the life that it seems to have. This one of Lu really speaks to me. Can you hear her, too?

MAKING REALISTIC SHOES

The following shoes, which are the ones that Lu is wearing, are quite time-consuming, but I think that they are worth the effort. The secret is to bake the foot form first, and then place the pieces of clay over the cooled form. It is almost like working with bits of leather, only they stretch—you don't have to sew them together!

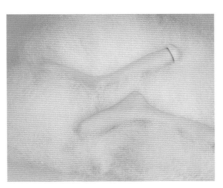

Bake the shoe and leg form.

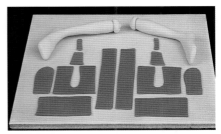

Cut pieces that you need to form parts of the shoe. No, I didn't dream these up myself! I copied the shapes from a favorite pair of my own shoes.

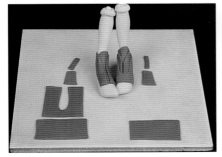

Add pieces to form, starting with the undermost layer.

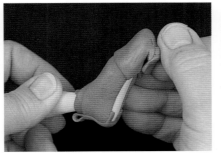

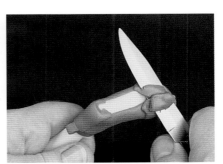

Stretch pieces around to the bottom of the shoe, and then cut off excess.

Press holes into shoes for laces.

Add stitch marks. You can do this with a sharp needle or with this wonderful wheel, called a *poncing tool*. I bought it at an art store.

If you wish to glue socks into the finished shoe, you will need to make room for them now. Here I am using a brush to pull the clay away from the ankle and foot.

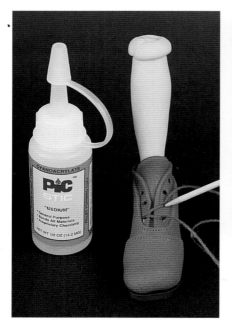

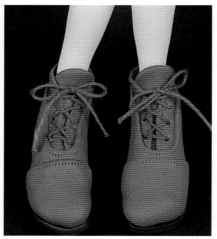

Bake the shoes. Cool, and then antique them with brown acrylic paint. Glue string into the holes for laces. A cyanoacrylate glue bonds very well with clay and dries quickly.

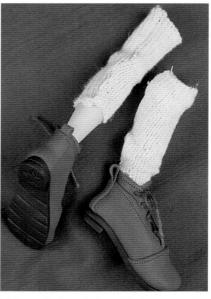

Make socks from lightweight knit material. Glue socks in place, pushing the bottom edge into the gap at top of shoes. A wet toothpick is a good tool for this.

MORE BUTTON-JOINT VARIATIONS

These little dolls have the same body as the larger dolls, but I skipped the cloth arms and legs and made solid clay ones. (Puppen FIMO with painted eyes and cheeks; 4" tall, seated.)

left: This close-up shows a bead being used instead of a button, but the principle is the same.

right: This doll is one of my alter egos. She is, in a sense, a caricature of me, even if she doesn't have my features; I see her as the calm part of me. Her hair is overspun wool from the loom of a beginning spinner: I love the texture.

This is Fear, whom we first met in chapter 2. Some days Fear hides in a pocket. Other days Fear is more brave. Either way the viewer is invited to interact. The button joints and floppy arms allow for this to be a very expressive doll, more so than if the arms were based on rigid wires. Fear is sewn into a pocket-type structure, thus there is no need of legs. The arms have only one joint. Otherwise this is very much a button-joint doll. Notice the polymer clay buttons. (Super Sculpey with painted eyes and eyebrows; 10½" tall to the tip of hat.)

Stick Puppet

I know that some of you really love to sculpt faces. And then you wonder what on earth you are going to do with them. You don't like to sew and stuff and make clothing, neither clay nor cloth! And about now you have a whole table full of heads. For you, I have a solution. Puppets!

The following pattern requires minimal sewing skills and can be easily adapted by adding trims, collars, a tie, buttons, ribbons, etc. Think of the outfit as a long coat, robe or shirt.

ADDITIONAL MATERIALS
- wooden dowels, size appropriate to size and weight of doll; Ruth, who is 17" tall, uses two ¼" dowels and one ⅜" dowel

SEWING STEPS
1. Add trim as desired to front and/or back of dress.
2. Sew shoulder seams.
3. Sew facing seams.
4. With right sides together, sew facing to neck of dress. Clip seams. Turn and press facing.
5. Sew side seams. Turn and press.
6. Hem bottom.

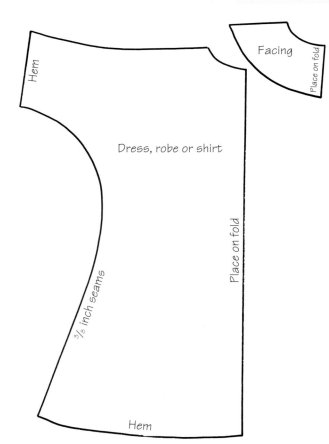

Puppet pattern. Enlarge the pattern to fit your doll.

Since Ruth (whom you met in chapter 2) is a very animated, active person, making her caricature into a puppet was a perfect choice.

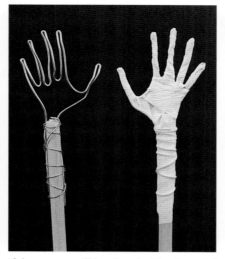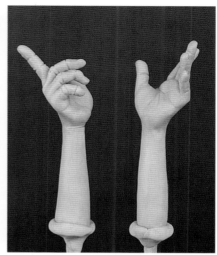

This is a straight-forward design: The head and hands are sculpted on dowels, in this case ¼" dowels for the hands and a stronger ⅜" dowel for the head.

If the puppet will be played with a lot, reinforce the fingers to make them stronger. Be sure to leave room for at least a 1⁄16" layer of clay over the hands. Clay stretched too thinly over wood may crack during baking. Be sure to bake thoroughly, since the wood may prevent the clay from heating evenly.

Gather the sleeve openings around the clay rings at the top of each arm. Sew the neck together to hide the ring. You're done! To manipulate the puppet, hold two dowels in one hand and one in the other.

Wire-Armature Dolls

There are many ways to make wire armatures for dolls. You can even buy them ready-made in doll supply catalogs. This method is the one I most frequently use. It is inexpensive yet sturdy, and custom-made to fit your doll.

STEPS FOR MAKING WIRE-ARMATURE DOLLS

First you will need to sculpt the parts for the doll. Sculpt each piece on a wire that is equal to two-thirds the height of the doll. For this project I am using the head sculpted in chapter 7. The hands were made with the same method used for Shandella.

ADDITIONAL MATERIALS
- quilt or craft batting or sweatsuit material (can be old fabric)
- lightweight knit material (can be an old T-shirt)

Follow with me, step by step, as we make this doll whom, in chapter 7, we called Milton.

These dolls, posing here in their underwear, represent the most frequently used type of armature for polymer clay dolls. Each is built on a wired "skeleton," which makes them poseable, flexible and very sturdy.

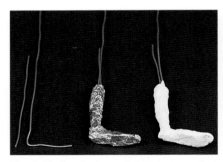

The foil helps the boots bake more evenly, and it cuts the cost of the clay. Once the foot is formed, it is covered with a layer of floral tape. Notice that there is a second small wire that is placed into the leg. This wire will later be removed and replaced with the U-wire.

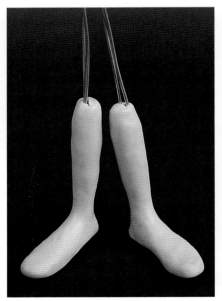

The armature is covered with clay until it is the desired shape and size. These legs will not show, so it is not necessary to get them completely smooth.

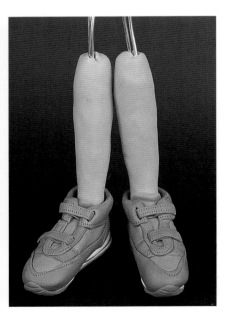

The shoes are built in layers in the same manner as Lu's. I copied an actual pair of my husband Dan's shoes.

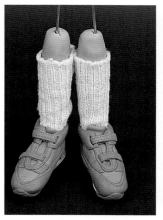

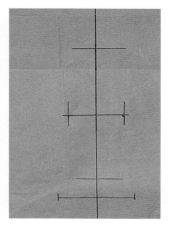

Make a stocking tube from an old stocking or a piece of knit material and glue it into the shoe.

On paper, draw a line to represent the doll's height, which in this case I wanted to be 16¾". Make five marks to designate the four sections of a person's body: top of head, nipples (or just below armpit), groin (or at bend of upper leg), bottom of knee and bottom of foot. Make a sixth mark to designate shoulders. Determine the width of the shoulders and hips. (Refer back to chapter 5 if you need help with body proportions.)

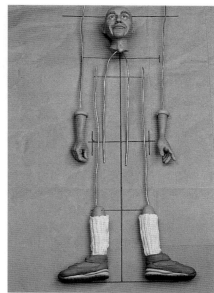

Lay the clay pieces on top of the diagram to see if all looks right.

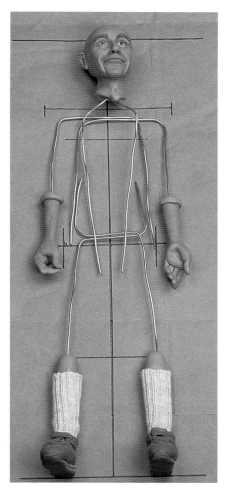

Bend arm wires at shoulders, and then cross them over the center and down the opposite side of the body. Bend leg wires at hip joint, and then cross them over the center and up the opposite side of the body.

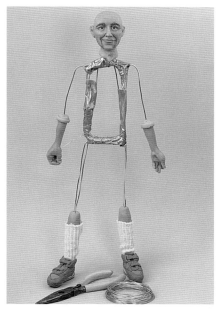

Use duct tape to secure wires in place. Cut a longer wire that, when bent into a U, will fit across the shoulders and into both shoes.

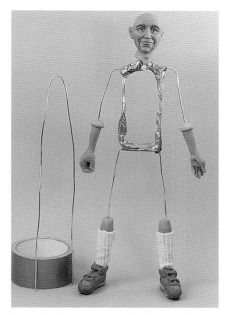

Press the U-wire into both shoes and tape in place. Secure all joined areas with wire; twist wire tightly at ends.

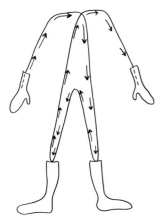

If a doll is larger than 18", and it is to stand, I suggest the addition of another wire to strengthen the armature. This is one continuous wire that is bent to fit the doll's proportions, and then taped and wired in place. The ends of this wire may be used to give extra support to the arms.

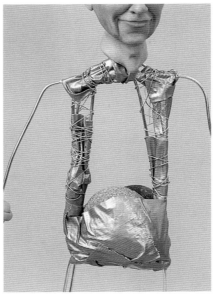

This next step is optional, but I love the way it adds weight plus a hidden "secret" to each doll. Find one or two small stones that fit into the body cavity of the doll. Write on them if you like, such as a special message for the owner of the doll or a favorite affirmation. Tape and then wire stones in place.

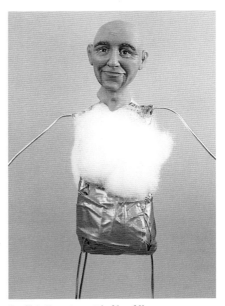

Stuff doll cavity with fiberfill.

Cut strips of batting and wrap doll tightly. For larger dolls, add fiberfill to thicker areas such as the thighs, buttocks and upper arms to eliminate the need for so much wrapping. Hold everything in place with more layers of wrapping material. Have a needle and thread handy with which to stitch loose areas in place.

Check the doll from all angles as you wrap to be sure the form is what you want.

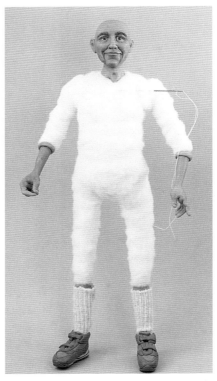

When you are happy with the shape, stitch through layers to keep them from slipping. If you are going to dress the doll in clothes that will never be removed, you can stop at this point and dress doll.

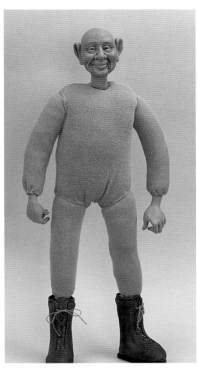

For a more finished doll, or for a doll that may be dressed and undressed, create a "skin" or underwear from a knit fabric. To make a pattern for this, pin a piece of paper toweling over the doll. Trace leg, arm and body shapes, leaving enough room for seams. Cut these out, and then stitch seams. Hand sew in place.

This doll is shaped with strips of sweatsuit material. Fiberfill was poked underneath the strips to provide "extra" shape.

This doll has a wire armature similar to the one we just made. I made her to represent my mother AnaBel. I don't view this as a caricature as much as an interpretation of my mother's essence. I love this doll: It represents the reason I make dolls.

Problems and Solutions

Hundreds of little clay people and character dolls have danced across my work table, investigated my oven and graced my shelves since 1979, when I first began using polymer clay. A number of these characters never quite got beyond the "making" stage, as something happened to short-circuit them directly into the garbage bin! But these hapless creations were not a total loss. From each of my mistakes, I learned something. I shared some of these lessons in my first North Light book, *How to Make Clay Characters*. Here are eight more "lessons" learned through the process of trial and error.

Clay Color and Baking

PROBLEM: The baked polymer clay skin color is not what you expected.

SOLUTION: Since clay does change color when it bakes, test bake a sample of your clay before sculpting.

At first glance, you may not see much difference between the top and bottom rows of the pictured clay buttons. But look again. The baked buttons on the bottom rows are darker and duller than the unbaked ones in the top rows. You can restore some of the sheen by polishing the baked clay. But if it is color you are after, you will have to choose the correct clay color before sculpting.

You can partially eliminate the problem by not baking the clay pieces quite so long or quite so hot. But polymer clay is stronger if it is thoroughly baked, which means at the highest recommended temperature for the longest recommended time. So, should you retain the raw clay color and risk a weak product, or bake the clay thoroughly and deal with color change?

I opt to bake thoroughly and deal with the color change, since it is very important to me to have a strong, reliable end product. To ensure I get the desired color, I test bake a piece of the chosen clay at the time and

The buttons in the top row are duplicates of the ones just below them in the bottom row, except that the top row is unbaked and the bottom row is baked. From left to right these clays are almond Cernit, caramel Cernit, nugget Cernit and terra cotta FIMO.

temperature I plan on baking the actual character. If I plan to do multiple bakings, I figure that in as well. Yes, this is a pain, but so is getting the wrong results.

For a lighter clay, add a bit of white clay to the mix. If a darker clay is the desired result, add dark brown or caramel clay. There may be a reddish tint in some of the dark brown mixes. To eliminate this, add a bit of green or navy blue. There may be a yellow tint in some of the caramel clays. To eliminate this, add a touch of red.

Another way to lighten the clay is to add a sizable portion of transparent clay. Just a little of the darker clays are enough to tint the transparent mix, since the pigment will more readily show through the transparent clays after they bake.

If you will antique or apply paint or chalk to your character, choose a flesh color slightly lighter than the desired end result. That way you can add the surface coloring, yet still get some natural skin variation.

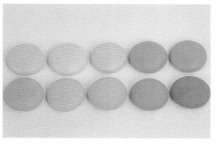

The buttons in the top row are duplicates of the ones just below them, except the top row is unbaked and the bottom row is baked. From left to right these clays are biscuit Cernit, flesh Cernit, flesh FIMO, Super Sculpey and beige Premo! Sculpey.

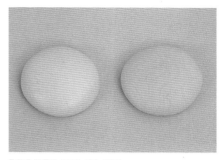

MARBLED CLAY
These two samples are made from the same mixture of FIMO and Cernit pink flesh-colored clays, but the left one is unbaked and the right is baked. If you look closely, you will see that the unbaked piece appears slightly marbled. However, if you weren't too particular, you could easily assume the two clays were mixed enough to begin sculpting. But see how much more the marbling shows up once the sample is baked. This clay should have been twisted and kneaded until there were absolutely no visible color variations.

Burned or Scorched Areas

PROBLEM: Uneven scorched areas.

SOLUTION: You can start over, you can camouflage with paint or you can bake with an awareness of scorching problems. The faces on these characters were baked at least three times, perhaps four, as I baked them in stages each time I added a new layer of clothing. I know that I should have baked these characters for only twenty minutes at perhaps 250°F during the first several bakes, and then baked them for the full time and at the highest recommended temperature during just the last bake.

The reason that I didn't do this is I am used to using FIMO, which generally is not too sensitive to the color changes that are brought on by long baking times. However, in this particular couple, I used FIMO that was mixed with Premo! Sculpey, which generally is more sensitive to color changes that are induced by heat. It is advisable to know the baking characteristics of each brand of polymer clay you use. What is true of one brand is not necessarily true of another. And don't mix brands in a bag unless you label it.

I worked several days on this couple, and loved the results except for the fact that the skin got progressively darker every time I baked the pieces. I ended up painting the woman's entire face with an opaque paint and then adding color. I tried to paint and blend the color on the man's nose to make it less evident.

In the close-up, even though I did camouflage the scorched nose with paint, it is still quite evident that this fellow's nose is a darker color than the rest of his face.

Mirror Sculpting

PROBLEM: The two sides of the face don't match.

SOLUTION: Turn the face upside down or look at it in a mirror so that you see the mirror image. Either method will allow you to look at the face with a new perspective and see things that you couldn't see before. I have sculpted enough faces now to know that I always, and I mean always, place the character's left eye closer to the bridge of the nose than the right eye. Yet I do not see this unevenness with my normal way of looking at the character! The only way that I can check for this is to do the upside-down or mirror-image thing. It's frustrating! But that is how I see. (I believe it is because my own face is asymmetrical, and unconsciously I create my sculptures in my own image. Perhaps you do the same? Check it out!)

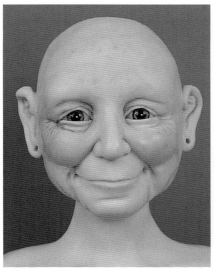

I really tried to get both sides of the face to match. Then I gave up and decided to leave her lopsided. How does she look to you? Look at the reversed image.

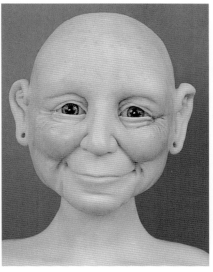

This is a reversed or mirror image of the same sculpture. Is it easier now to tell which parts of her face are asymmetrical?

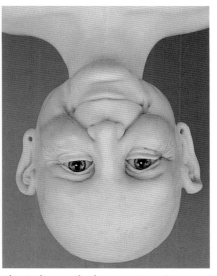

This is the upside-down version. Can you see how one side of her face is different from the other?

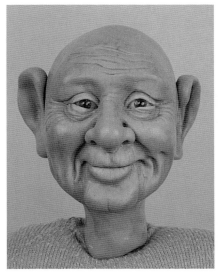

Try the same process with this character. This is the normal image.

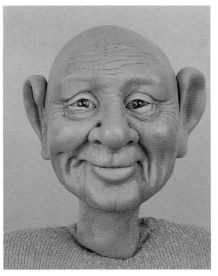

This is the mirror or reversed image.

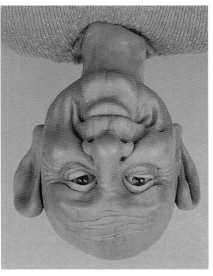

And, of course, this one is upside down.

Cracks or Checks in the Baked Surface

PROBLEM: Cracks or under-the-surface checks appear in the baked clay.

SOLUTION: Try to eliminate the source, which is usually one of these things: trapped air, trapped moisture or uneven clay thickness. Eliminate moisture problems by keeping the clay tightly wrapped and away from areas of high humidity. This may not be possible. The next choice is to be watchful for evidence of trapped air or moisture. This usually shows up in the unbaked clay as lighter-colored bubbles under the surface. If you spot these bubbles, work them out with your finger or by slicing the area with a very sharp blade and then reblending it.

Sometimes you do everything that you can and these irregular spots still show up—and in areas where they are very visible. If that happens, try camouflaging them with paint or freckles. If this isn't possible, try a little doll surgery as shown in the pictures.

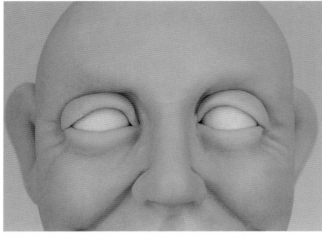

All looked well with Annie until I baked her, and then that crack showed up right between her eyes.

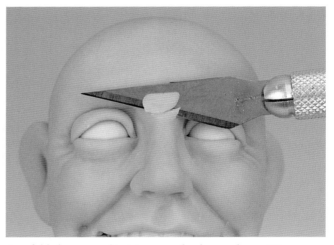

A craft blade was used to trim away the damaged area. Warm polymer clay is easier to cut than cold clay is, so warm the head in the oven before doing surgery. Be careful with the rest of the head, as thin areas like ears will be fragile when they are warm.

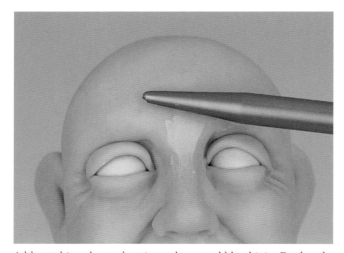

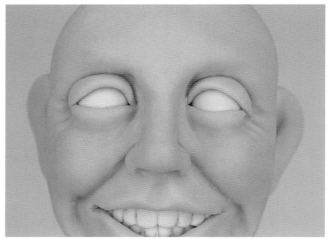

Add matching clay to the trimmed area and blend it in. Feather the edges with a brush and your finger tips. The waterless hand cleaner also works well for smoothing the edges. See next page for baking directions.

Adding Raw Clay to Baked Clay

PROBLEM: Getting a reliable bond between baked and unbaked clay.

SOLUTION: Use a cyanoacrylate glue as a bonding agent. I was planning to use this head with a wire armature. For this, it did not need a ring around its neck. But then I decided to make it into a bolster doll, which required a ring to hold up the dress. And it needed to be very secure. I made the clay ring, and then stuck it to the baked neck with a thin application of cyanoacrylate glue. Once the glue is applied, don't tamper with the bond.

BAKING DIRECTIONS

In order to adequately cure this new clay, bake the piece at the highest recommended temperature for the longest recommended time. If you are concerned about color changes in the clay, start the clay at a lower temperature than the recommended high and bake for fifteen minutes, and then raise the temperature to the highest recommended temperature and bake fifteen minutes more. Be aware there are variables in this due to the mass of the head, the type of clay and how much clay is added. So keep an eye on your piece. Camouflage any differences in color with paint. Check out finished Annie in chapter 8. Did you notice any problems in this area of her forehead?

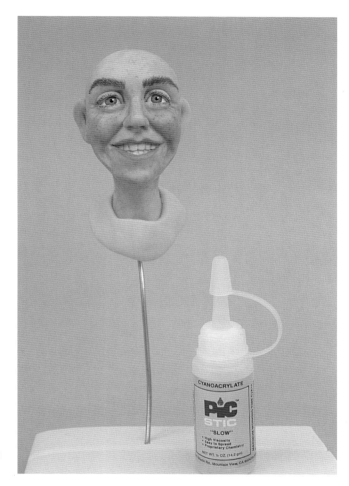

Sculpting With Very Soft Clay

PROBLEM: Very soft clay makes sculpting too difficult to get correct form.

SOLUTION: Bake the piece, and then make corrections.

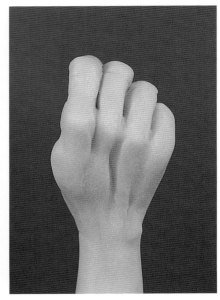

Soft clay gives and moves, but it does not push back. This pushing back or resistance is sometimes needed to finish a piece. That is what happened with these hands. When I tried to fill the dip in the top of the finger or the cavity in the back of the hands, the whole hand distorted. The solutions was to bake the hand as it was, even though I wasn't happy with it.

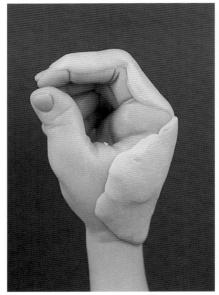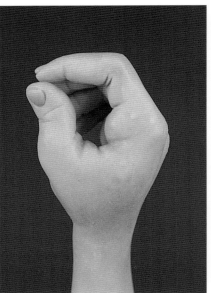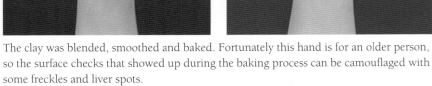

Now that the hand is baked, I can handle it without distorting its shape. I added raw clay to the hand to fill in the misshapen areas.

The clay was blended, smoothed and baked. Fortunately this hand is for an older person, so the surface checks that showed up during the baking process can be camouflaged with some freckles and liver spots.

Propping Characters in the Oven

PROBLEM: Difficult to prop pieces.

SOLUTION: Be creative! There are many ways to do this.

This character has very large hands that will droop during the baking process unless they are supported. I need them to stay in this exact position so that they can later hold some juggling balls. The solution was to make a support from a piece of clay, a dowel and some stiff paper. The T-pin was used to keep it all steady.

Standing characters always need to be supported unless their base is weighted enough to prevent them from tipping. This one is prone to tipping, so I used a wire to attach him to the mug. The handle of the mug keeps him from tipping backward. The index card keeps the handle from leaving a shiny spot on his coat.

After he cools, I add his head and the juggling balls. It is tempting to think of him as being stable, as he now stands quite firmly. However, I know that the heat of the oven will make him vulnerable to tipping. His coat has been baked and is quite solid around his chest, so I now use a space under his arms around which to wrap the wire. I use the same support for his hands as I did the first time that he was baked.

Rose needs no support for her body as she is sitting, but her hands and the mug need support. For this I use the same support as I did for the juggler.

I add the little Mug Dweller to the baked mug and rebake the whole character, again using the hand support.

Finishing the Eyes

PROBLEM: Have difficulty painting eyes. Is there another solution?

SOLUTION: You certainly don't have to paint eyes if you hate doing so. There are alternatives:

• A helpful and talented friend!
This is the ideal solution, but I find that very few people love to paint eyes. We do so because we like the results. But if you can find a painting friend, go for it!

• Black glass or stone beads
These are especially useful for small figures, where the eyes are so small that the painting doesn't show much anyway. They also are effective in smiling characters where the eyes squint almost shut.

• Acrylic eyes
Good-quality acrylic eyes can be baked in the oven if you use care. I frequently use these in doll classes because they are relatively inexpensive and they give great immediate results. The problem is that sometimes the surface will crack during the baking process. If this happens, apply a coat of polymer-safe lacquer or varnish. This will sometimes disguise the crack. I use the lacquer that is produced by Eberhard Faber for FIMO. I used acrylic eyes for all three of the wire armature dolls in chapter 8 who are pictured in their "underwear."

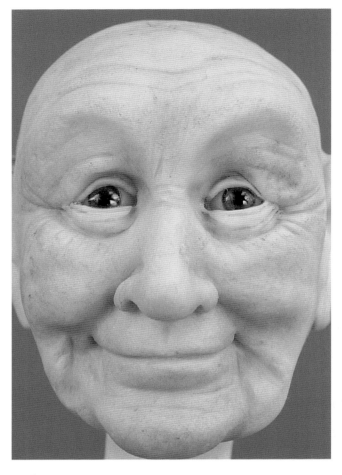

If you look carefully you will notice a crack in this fellow's acrylic eyes. This happens sometimes during baking.

• Glass eyes
Glass eyes, though expensive, are ideal. Use them for your more time-intensive creations. The only drawback that I know of on glass eyes, besides the cost, is that often the irises are large in proportion to the size of the eye. (This is also true of the acrylic eyes.) Thus the eyes of dolls with less than wide-open eyes may appear to be all iris, with tiny whites.

Books! What a treasure! The following books have been very valuable to me in my career and in getting together information for this book. The starred ones have been especially helpful and are recommended if you would like more understanding of the nuances involved in "seeing" the human form.

DOLL- AND FIGURE-MAKING BOOKS

Carlson, Maureen. *How to Make Clay Characters*. North Light Books, 1507 Dana Ave., Cincinnati, OH 45207. 1997.

Dodge, Venus. *The Doll's Dressmaker*. Sterling Publishing Co. Inc., 2 Park Ave., New York, NY 10016. 1987.

Oroyan, Susanna. *Anatomy of a Doll* (and other related titles). C&T Publishing, P.O. Box 1456, Lafayette, CA 94549. 1997.

DRAWING AND ANATOMY BOOKS

Faigan, Gary. *Facial Expressions*. Watson-Guptill Publications, 1515 Broadway, New York, NY 10036. 1990.

Gautier, Dick. *Drawing and Cartooning 1,001 Caricatures*. The Berkeley Publishing Group, 200 Madison Ave., New York, NY 10016. 1995.

Hamm, Jack. *Drawing the Head and Figure*. The Putnam Publishing Group, 200 Madison Ave., New York, NY 10016. 1963.

Peck, Stephen Rogers. *Atlas of Human Anatomy*. Oxford University Press, New York, NY. 1951.

Redman, Lenn. *How to Draw Caricatures*. Contemporary Books, Inc., 180 N. Michigan Ave., Chicago, IL 60610. 1984.

POLYMER CLAY BOOKS

Kalinski, Mary. *Making Miniatures in Polymer Clay*. Scott Publications, 30595 Eight Mile, Livonia, MI 48152-1798.

Kato, Donna. *The Art of Polymer Clay*. Watson-Guptill Publications, 1515 Broadway, New York, NY 10036. 1997.

Roche, Nan. *The New Clay*. Flower Valley Press, 4806 Camelot St., Rockville, MD 20853. 1991.

POLYMER CLAY SUPPLIES

Polymer clay has become a staple arts and crafts material in arts and crafts stores, mail-order catalogs and on Websites throughout the United States. If you cannot find polymer clay in your area, contact:

Wee Folk Creations

18476 Natchez Avenue
Prior Lake, MN 55372
(612) 447-3828
For orders: (888-WEE-FOLK)
Fax: (612) 447-8816
E-mail: weefolk@weefolk.com
http://www.weefolk.com

FIBER FOR DOLL HAIR

The Fiber Studio

P.O. Box 637
Henniker, NH 03242
(603) 428-7830
E-mail: sales@fiberstudio.com
http://www.fiberstudio.com
Specializes in Tibetan wool (on the skin), mohair, specialty wools and other natural fibers.

One & Only Creations

P.O. Box 2730
Napa, CA 94558
(800) 262-6768
http://www.oneandonlycreations.com
Call or write for a free full-color catalogue. Specializes in specialty and natural fibers.

DOLL EYES

G Schoepfer, Inc.

460 Cook Hill Road
Cheshire, CT 06410
(203) 250-7796
For orders only: (800) 875-6939
Fax: (203) 250-7796
Carries glass and acrylic eyes.

POLYMER CLAY ORGANIZATIONS

National Polymer Clay Guild

PMB 345
1350 Beverly Road, 115
McLean, VA 22101
http://www.npcg.org
This nonprofit organization puts out a bimonthly newsletter that is well worth the price of membership for those wishing to keep updated on what is happening in the world of polymer clay.

INDEX